CYCLING IN
THE COTSWOLDS

by Chiz Dakin

2 POLICE SQUARE, MILNTHORPE, CUMBRIA LA7 7PY
www.cicerone.co.uk

Printed in China on behalf of Latitude Press Ltd.
A catalogue record for this book is available from the British Library.
All photographs are by the author unless otherwise stated.

 This product includes mapping data licensed from Ordnance
Survey® with the permission of the Controller of Her
Majesty's Stationery Office. © Crown copyright 2014. All
 rights reserved. Licence number PU100012932.
Base maps by Lovell Johns www.lovelljohns.co.uk

Acknowledgements

As ever there are far too many people to thank for all the help – big and
small – I've had along the way, but without the support of my wonderful
husband Reuben this project would have been very much harder. Thanks
also to everyone who tirelessly answered my queries on subjects such
as obscure rights of way and the new Sustrans Two Tunnels route, and to
my friends Patrick and Jessica Wooddisse for local info in the southern
Cotswolds (and for coming out on a ride or two with me) and to sister-
in-law Jo (in Stratford) for the coffees. A big thanks also to the Lion Inn in
Winchcombe and the Old Brewhouse B&B in Cirencester for helping me
keep my own costs to a minimum while researching the multiday route: I'd
happily recommend them both, regardless of their help.

Advice to Readers

While every effort is made by our authors to ensure the accuracy of guidebooks as
they go to print, changes can occur during the lifetime of an edition. If we know
of any, there will be an Updates tab on this book's page on the Cicerone website
(www.cicerone.co.uk), so please check before planning your trip. We also advise
that you check information about such things as transport, accommodation and
shops locally. Even rights of way can be altered over time. We are always grateful
for information about any discrepancies between a guidebook and the facts on
the ground, sent by email to info@cicerone.co.uk or by post to Cicerone, 2 Police
Square, Milnthorpe LA7 7PY, United Kingdom.

Front cover: In summer, the ford at Upper Slaughter is just the right depth for a
cooling splash-through!

CONTENTS

Map key 6
Overview map 7

INTRODUCTION 9
Geology 11
Wildlife, plants and flowers 12
History 13
Art, culture and local festivities. 14
Food and drink 15
Getting around 16
When to go 17
Accommodation. 18
What to wear 19
What to take. 20
Maps 21
Waymarking and access 21
Cycling efficiently. 24
How hard are the routes? 25
Using this guide 28

Route 1   Shipston-on-Stour Loop via Brailes Hill. 31
Route 2   Shipston-on-Stour Loop via Halford 35
Route 3   Shipton-under-Wychwood Loop via Wychwood 40
Route 4   Bourton-on-the-Water Loop via the Slaughters 44
Route 5   Alderton via Broadway 49
Route 6   Bradford-on-Avon via Bath Two Tunnels 54
Route 7   Bourton-on-the-Water Loop via Great Barrington 60
Route 8   Kemble via Cotswold Water Park. 65
Route 9   Kingham Loop via Bruern Abbey. 70
Route 10   Batheaston Sting 76
Route 11   Stratford Greenway Loop via Mickleton 80
Route 12   Cirencester Loop via Ampney Crucis. 85
Route 13   Filkins Loop via Bibury 90
Route 14   Fairford Loop via Bibury 96
Route 15   Frampton Cotterell Loop via Wickwar 101
Route 16   Stonehouse Loop via Slimbridge 108
Route 17   Stow Loop via Blockley. 115
Route 18   Burford Loop via Northleach. 122
Route 19   Stroud Loop via Chavenage House 129
Route 20   Cheltenham Loop via Cleeve Hill 139

Route 21   Malmesbury Loop via Tetbury 147
Route 22   Around the Cotswolds. 154
           Day 1 Stroud to Winchcombe 156
           Day 2 Winchcombe to Stow-on-the-Wold. 163
           Day 3 Stow-on-the-Wold to Cirencester 171
           Day 4 Cirencester to Stroud. 181

Appendix A   Route summary table 189
Appendix B   Cycle hire and cycle shops 191
Appendix C   Cycles and trains 195
Appendix D   First aid for bike and rider. 197
Appendix E   Other useful information 201

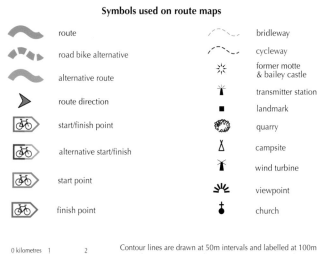

Symbols used on route maps

route   bridleway
road bike alternative   cycleway
alternative route   former motte & bailey castle
route direction   transmitter station
start/finish point   landmark
alternative start/finish   quarry
start point   campsite
finish point   wind turbine
                                    viewpoint
                                    church

0 kilometres   1   2
0 miles   1

Contour lines are drawn at 50m intervals and labelled at 100m intervals. Route maps are drawn at 1:100,000 (1cm = 1km) except for the Route 22 overview map which is at 1:250,000.

Features on the overview map

County/Unitary boundary
Urban area
National Park eg **BRECON BEACONS**
Area of Outstanding Natural
Beauty, eg *The Cotswolds*

600m
400m
200m
75m
0m

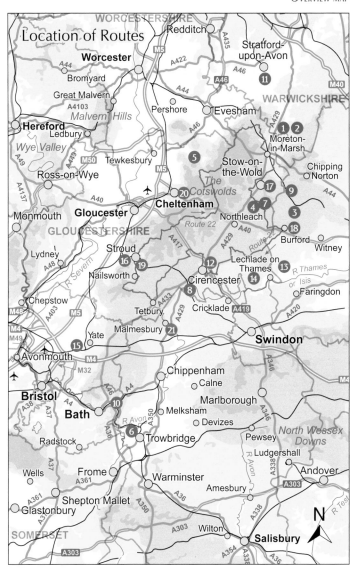

In spring, apple blossom lines part of the bridleway near Furze Ground (Route 13)

INTRODUCTION

A typical eastern Cotswold view over ripening corn and rolling hills – near Chadlington (Route 9)

The track in front of me was smooth, dry and flat and there wasn't another soul in sight. To my right the mirror-calm water reflected the blue skies overhead, with a few fluffy white clouds adding extra interest. Splashes of colour from brightly-painted canal boats and tall, motionless green spikes of bankside vegetation added to the tranquil scene. I was on the Stroudwater Canal near Slimbridge (Route 16) and had stopped to take some photos of the peaceful early-morning scene. A moment later I was particularly glad I hadn't just hurtled by at speed...

A swan was snoozing quietly in the shade of tall reeds, all curled up with her sinuous head buried beneath a wing, now and again raising it drowsily at some gentle background noise. As I was about to edge past her, another early-morning cyclist arrived rather abruptly, seeing the swan (and me waving my arms) only at the last minute. He then rode carefully past this sleepy queen of the canal, keeping as far away as he could. But we needn't have worried: she was far more concerned about catching up on her beauty sleep than hissing territorially at either of us.

On another occasion I was pedalling as fast as I could up a steep but short slope; that day I was on an off-road section of Akeman Street (Route

Cotswold stone houses beside the River Eye in Lower Slaughter (Route 4)

18), grinning from ear to ear as I overcame a challenge that looked more difficult than it was in practice.

Such is the variety of terrain in the Cotswolds, from quiet lanes and challenging tracks to thriving (and busy) villages and town centres. And unexpected wildlife encounters seem far more common when travelling by bicycle – the quiet but relatively fast approach on two wheels allowing you to get a bit closer than perhaps by any other means of transport, including feet.

The Cotswolds are deservedly one of the most popular Areas of Outstanding National Beauty (AONB) in the country, and its honeypot (and honey-coloured) limestone villages and wool towns such as Bourton-on-the-Water, Broadway and Bibury are the embodiment of 'olde-worlde' rural England. Although summer tourists can make these places very busy, the bustle can soon be left behind on the quiet lanes and tracks that criss-cross this wonderfully varied region, passing such delights as purple lavender fields and swathes of wildflowers peppering the unimproved limestone grassland.

These, and the relatively gentle terrain, really lend the Cotswolds to cycling. But make no mistake: it's not flat! There are plenty of hills here, often gentle and rolling in nature, although some are surprisingly steep – they just don't ascend to such lofty heights as some of the more renowned hilly areas of the UK.

The routes in this book cover between 14km (9 miles) and 64km (40 miles) in a day, leading up to a 208km (130 miles) four-day route that visits many Cotswold highlights.

GEOLOGY

In the Jurassic Period (roughly 200–145 million years ago), the land that now forms the Cotswold Hills was in the tropics and completely underwater. The depth of these tropical seas varied over time, with the deeper waters producing thick clays and the shallower seas forming limestone from the shells of marine creatures living and dying in the waters.

More recently (geologically speaking) the land has tilted, leading to a steep scarp slope on the northwest edge of the region and rolling hills towards the south and east. This is illustrated in the steep slopes above Cheltenham (Route 20) and the gentler, plateau-like terrain above the Slaughters (Route 4).

The clay rocks are known as 'Lias' – a term invented by 18th-century quarry workers to describe the layered rock, and adopted by William Smith, a canal-building engineer who went on to become the 'Father of Geology' (See Route 9 for more on William Smith). The limestone is Oolitic – where the regular structure of spherical crystals looks like a collection of eggs. This is divided into two groups: Inferior Oolites are the older of the two, and tend to be found on the scarp slopes of the northwest Cotswolds; Greater Oolites are more typically found on the gentler slopes outside the north west, and form the region's traditional honey-coloured building limestone, the colour being typically more pronounced towards the north of the region. Its evenness of grain (enabling it to be cut in any direction) and durability made it the preferred building stone for many

Rolling hillside east of the scarp edge near Snowshill (Route 22, Day 2)

prestigious buildings, such as St Paul's Cathedral.

Glacial and post-glacial meltwater rivers have also contributed to the sometimes surprisingly hilly nature of the Cotswolds – with the Stroud valleys (Routes 19 and 22) being good examples of deeply-incised river valleys in the region.

The greater presence of clays to the south end of the Cotswolds means there is a greater chance here of encountering boggy, slow-drying ground; when these begin to 'bog out' or flood, routes in the north are more likely to still be rideable.

This heron on the Kennet and Avon Canal seems remarkably unafraid of humans (Route 6)

WILDLIFE, PLANTS AND FLOWERS

The Cotswolds area is of national importance for some of the smaller and shyer species of wildlife. The watercourses in particular are among the last remaining strongholds of the nationally scarce water vole, although even here it is a rare sighting. Otters are beginning to make a comeback along the headwaters of the Thames; dragon and damselflies are rather more common sightings.

On dry land, hares and fallow deer are frequent sightings; less common are glimpses of weasels, badgers and foxes. Unimproved grassland, hay meadows and common areas are often host to sunbathing adders and all sorts of butterflies, including several varieties of fritillary and blue butterflies.

Birdwatchers may get frequent sightings of the red kite, or a more commonplace buzzard circling overhead. Skylarks warble high in the sky, with swallows performing acrobatic displays at a lower altitude, and herons can sometimes be seen on the banks of canals and rivers.

Ancient beech woodland can be found along the scarp slopes near Winchcombe; other common trees throughout the Cotswolds include oak, ash, hawthorn, willow, maple and hazel. Traditionally these (willow in particular) were coppiced or pollarded.

In spring, pungent white flowers of wild garlic or a blue-purple carpet of bluebells (often both together) cover the floors of limestone woodlands. Come summer, prolific wildflowers such as blue meadow cranesbill (wild geraniums) and orchids, and common buttercups and daisies, adorn the grassy verges.

The fields near Snowshill (Route 22) are transformed when the lavender comes out in late summer

In fields, green or golden cereals and the bright yellow of oil-seed rape are commonplace, with two less-common crops being the purple flowers of flax and lavender. If you're lucky you may see bright splashes of red where poppies have grown among the crops.

HISTORY

The Cotswolds have a long history of human settlement, with a few early finds dating back to the Stone Age. However, the earliest records of widespread settlement in the region begin around 4000BC in the Neolithic era (the late Stone Age). Some places, such as Salmondsbury Site of Special Scientific Interest (SSSI) near

Bourton-on-the-Water (Routes 4 and 7) are thought to have been farmed continuously since that time. Burial chambers from Neolithic to Roman times are commonplace – such as the long barrows of Belas Knap (near Route 22, Day 1) and Hetty Pegler's Tump (close to Route 16).

The Romans left many signs of their presence in the 1st to 5th centuries: Corinium forms the basis of modern-day Cirencester; the remnants of several Roman roads such as the Fosse Way and Ryknield Street still criss-cross the region; and archaeological evidence suggests several wealthy Romans had villas in the region. When the Romans eventually went south, Angles and (more often) Saxons moved in, with Alfred

Northleach was granted a market charter in AD1227 (Route 18)

the Great (of Wessex) and Aethelstan (the first King of England) being of notable mention.

During the late Dark and early Middle Ages the region became wealthy from sheep-farming, particularly after fuller's earth – a local type of clay rich in silica – was discovered to be excellent for removing grease from raw fleece. The wool merchants spent some of their considerable wealth on restoring or rebuilding the market towns and churches of the region.

In the 18th and 19th centuries transport routes by canal and railway grew rapidly across the region, but little new industry was attracted as the area had no nearby source of coal for power. Nowadays the major industries are tourism and agriculture.

ART, CULTURE AND LOCAL FESTIVITIES

With the home of Shakespeare to the north and the Georgian grandeur of Bath to the south, it should come as no surprise that the Cotswolds are home to a thriving cultural scene. Tourist information centres and online websites (see Appendix E) are good sources of information for current events. Local magazines such as *Cotswold Life* also highlight upcoming events.

The more unusual events in the region include:

- Tetbury Woolsack Races (May), where contestants race between two pubs, up and down a hill with a 1:4 gradient, while carrying a 60lb sack of wool.
- Robert Dover's Cotswold Olimpicks (May), where the highlight of events is shin-kicking.

One of the organisers of the Tetbury Woolsack Races lifts the 60lb woolsack onto his upper back – the position most contestants use to run with it

This version of the Olympic games has been going for over 400 years.

- Cooper's Hill Cheese Rolling Festival (May/June), where contestants chase a Double Gloucester cheese down a hill whose gradient approaches 1:1.
- Bourton-on-the Water river football (August), where the shin-deep river forms the pitch and goalposts are set up under the bridges.
- Morris dancing can be seen throughout the year, often in busier tourist towns and villages. Its origins are lost in time, but two main theories suggest either it started as a fertility ritual or as a war dance.
- Stow-on-the-Wold's Gypsy Horse Fairs in May and October.

- Levellers Day in Burford (May) celebrates a 1649 pro-democracy demonstration against Cromwell by some of his New Model Army.

FOOD AND DRINK

In a region that owes much of its former prosperity to wool, it should come as no surprise that lamb is a local speciality. The 'Cotswold Lion' sheep, introduced by the Romans, produces very fine-quality wool, and its meat tends to be milder and less 'gamey' than other breeds. Another speciality is Gloucestershire Old Spot pork, whether as a sausage cob from Huffkins in Burford (Route 18) or as a full-blown pork belly dinner at the Slaughters Country Inn (Route 4).

On the northern edge of the Cotswolds is the Vale of Evesham,

Local treats worth burning some calories for: asparagus, a Cotswold cream tea and a pint of local real ale

widely regarded as the fruit and vegetable basket of Britain. Asparagus and soft tree fruits are specialities that make their way into many Cotswolds recipes.

The olde worlde Englishness typical of Cotswolds villages lends itself to a time-honoured tradition: the cream tea. A well-earned treat after a good workout on the bike!

The region has a thriving real ale scene with too many microbreweries to mention. Wychwood and Hook Norton are the larger and better-known breweries (Wadworth's also historically brewed in Burford). Lesser-known breweries include Donnington (near Stow), Goffs (near Winchcombe), Cotswold Lion (near Cheltenham) and Stroud (in Stroud, naturally).

As usual in the UK, wine aficionados have few local choices, but of note is the Co-op's recent (2010) establishment of a vineyard near Cirencester, beside woods believed to be a former Roman vineyard. Their first batch of wine is due to market in 2014.

GETTING AROUND

By train

Travellers intending to use trains to get around the region should read Appendix C for more information on relevant train operating companies and their main requirements in relation to carrying bikes. The main routes run from Birmingham to Bristol (via Cheltenham); Swindon to Cheltenham; Oxford to Worcester; Birmingham to Stratford; and Worcester to Stratford.

By car

Parking in the Cotswolds is strictly controlled in many places, both in pay and display car parks and on the roadside. However, it is often possible to find free parking close to many of the routes – just ensure that any vehicle is parked legally and with consideration for residents, who have to put up with visitors invading their world every summer! Also remember that farmers often need spontaneous access to apparently overgrown field entrances, and that agricultural vehicles may need a wide turning circle close to and opposite gates.

Individual route descriptions suggest parking options available locally. Further parking information can be found online at Transport Direct www.transportdirect.info or Parkopedia www.parkopedia.co.uk.

WHEN TO GO

The best time to cycle in the Cotswolds is in early summer. Throughout the summer, days are longer, the weather is warmer (if not always sunnier!) and routes tend to be much less muddy than in winter. On the downside, accommodation and transport are busier, more expensive and get booked up earlier; vegetation begins to invade paths; and popular centres such as Bourton-on-the-Water, Broadway, Bibury and Winchcombe can get heaving (especially at weekends). However, peace and quiet can be found just a couple of kilometres away from these places – even in midsummer.

Early autumn and late spring can also offer great cycling: the weather can often be dry and sunny (if windy); the days are still reasonably long and vegetation is less of an issue. Accommodation is cheaper and less busy than in summer, as are trains and tourist centres, but festivals are fewer.

But beware the Jekyll-and-Hyde nature of off-road surfaces. When dry,

In autumn, the leaves of many of the local trees turn a fantastic shade of red. These are Acer (maple) trees at the world-renowned Westonbirt Arboretum near Malmesbury (near Route 21)

the trails are hard-baked and although they may be bouncy or even bone-shaking they usually offer a relatively easy-going surface. Light or short-lived rain will not have a major effect on this once the ground has dried out in spring. Once wet-through, however, the surface can acquire the thick gloopy consistency of a bog, and may flood.

Unless you like thick, clarty, dauby sticky stuff, winter is definitely not recommended for the novice cyclist, and even the more experienced cyclist may wish to stick more to the roads. However, for the experienced and prepared cyclist, particularly one who enjoys a thoroughly muddy off-road challenge, winter offers a quiet and adventurous angle to a cycling visit to the Cotswolds.

All of the route descriptions in this book assume dry summer conditions.

ACCOMMODATION

Accommodation is widely available throughout the Cotswolds, although there are only a few hostels. Due to its popularity with tourists, the region's hotels and B&Bs can seem quite expensive, especially in the summer season. The high demand for rooms during this time means it's best to book your bed well in advance.

Many accommodation providers in the more remote areas assume arrival by car, which isn't always helpful for cyclists. It's also worth bearing in mind that some of the smaller villages may have just one option, or even none at all, for accommodation and refreshments. Appendix E contains details of websites that are useful for researching and booking accommodation in the Cotswolds, including websites that provide information specifically on cycle-friendly accommodation. A number of establishments in the area have cycle-friendly accreditation, but wherever you decide to stay it's advisable to check before booking that there will be somewhere safe to store your bike overnight and facilities for drying wet gear.

Bases of a reasonable size from which to explore the Cotswolds include (roughly south to north):
- Bath, Bradford on Avon or Bristol (Routes 6, 10 and 15)
- Cirencester or Stroud (Routes 8, 12, 13, 14, 16, 19 and 22)
- Bourton-on-the-Water or Stow-on-the-Wold (Routes 3, 4, 7, 9, 17, 18 and 22)
- Cheltenham or Tewkesbury (Routes 5, 20 and 22)
- Chipping Campden or Shipston-on-Stour (Routes 1, 2, 7, 17 and 22)
- Stratford-upon-Avon (1, 2, 11 and 22).

A good starting point for your accommodation search is www.cyclistswelcome.co.uk – the Cyclists' Touring Club's (CTC's) list of cycle-friendly accommodation. For a more general search try www.cotswolds.com.

WHAT TO WEAR

Newcomers to cycling would be forgiven for thinking head-to-toe Lycra in lurid colours is essential, judging by the attire of some road cycling clubs. Fortunately this is not the case, although there are certain items of clothing that will make your ride more comfortable and therefore more enjoyable.

Cycling shorts

Cycling (padded) shorts make life on the bike much more comfortable, particularly for those new to cycling or on longer routes. These do not need to be your only layer – they easily fit underneath most pairs of more stylish and loose-fitting shorts (many shorts aimed at mountain bikers are designed in this way). You can also get padded cycling underwear if you prefer the two-layer approach. Most cyclists wouldn't ride without some form of proper cycling shorts!

Breathable upper and lower outer layers

The British weather can change notoriously quickly, especially on higher ground, and a sunny day can quickly become windy and wet. The number and type of layers you should wear will depend on the time of year, but be careful not to overburden yourself. This is very much a personal preference, but as a minimum a lightweight, breathable and quick-drying jacket that is both windproof and waterproof will make poor weather (expected or not) much more bearable. If it is also in a hi-visibility colour such as yellow or orange, with reflective patches, it will improve your safety for no extra weight. Breathability is important to allow sweat created going uphill (or into strong winds) to escape.

Trouser legs should ideally be close-fitting, particularly around the ankles, to avoid catching in the chain ring. If they are not, tuck them into your socks.

Cycling gloves

Shock-absorbing patches in the palms offer more comfort to your arms, particularly on off-road sections where vibrations are more intense. Outside the summer season your hands will chill surprisingly quickly in wet or cool conditions; full-fingered waterproof gloves are therefore preferable.

Shades

These are extremely useful – even on a rainy day. As well as reducing glare from bright or low sun, they also keep flying insects, mud and driving rain out of your eyes. Some cyclists wear clear shades on every ride.

Cycling shoes/clip-in pedals

It's worthwhile wearing cycle shoes. They may look like normal trainers or leisure shoes, but they have stiffened soles that prevent foot pain and long-term problems associated with the concentrated pressure of cycling.

As your cycling progresses and you tackle longer and harder routes,

Stiff cycling shoes are useful, but adding SPD plates to 'clip in' is best left until you're sure it's worth the money and the time getting used to them

clip-in pedals may become worthwhile. These positively lock your feet to the pedals, requiring a heel-twist to unlock. Besides keeping feet secure on rough ground, they allow you to pull up on the pedals as well as pushing down.

Most cycle shoes feature attachment points for the shoe cleats, which are supplied with the pedals, so clip-in pedals can be added later. However, the 'locked-in' feeling can be unnerving if you are not used to it, so only make this progression when you are confident.

Which type of bike?

Nearly all the routes in this book could be done on road bikes, in which case you will need to follow the on-road detours marked on the maps and highlighted in the sidebar beside some route descriptions. But you'll have more fun, and be able to explore quieter trails and tracks, if you're prepared to take a mountain bike or a hybrid (or 'sturdy') bike, which will manage the off-road sections fine in dry conditions. In wet conditions, the best bike to take, if you wish to tackle the off-road sections, will be a mountain bike.

Other basic equipment

Reputable cycle hire centres will usually provide you with a lock, pump and helmet free of charge. Most will also provide a small repair kit (enough to change an inner tube), but you may well have to ask for this. A lock is a good idea if you plan to leave your cycle unattended.

Although many hire centres will encourage you to wear a helmet, there is no requirement under UK law to wear one and it is entirely up to individual cyclists to decide for themselves. Parents should bear in mind younger children's vulnerability and instability; protective gear comes in all shapes and colours these days and will not necessarily seem 'uncool' or off-putting to young people.

Toolkit

Appendix D contains detailed information about the tools you might need on a cycle trip – including a step-by-step puncture repair guide.

Water bottles

These (one or two, depending on route length) can be held in frame-mounted bottle cages.

Luggage

Although it is possible to carry day kit in a small rucksack, it is much more pleasant and comfortable to carry things in a handlebar bag, rear rack bag or (for larger loads) panniers. Handlebar bags with a clear top pocket to carry a map can be particularly useful. If you use electronic rather than paper maps you may prefer the type that securely holds a small tablet. Smartphone apps (such as Strava or MapMyRide) for cycling are becoming increasingly common; they provide electronic mapping and a log (along with stats) of your route, and they may well become the norm in the future. But beware: satellite GPS eats batteries. Many cyclists also complain of poor visibility in bright light, and smartphones are expensive to replace if damaged by rain, mud or falls.

All luggage should be properly and securely fitted using appropriate brackets, with panniers also requiring a rear rack. Beware of wheels becoming snagged by loose straps or floppy panniers.

The size of this book constrains the scale of mapping that can be used within it; as such, it is advisable to take with you some form of larger-scale mapping, such as Ordnance Survey (OS) 1:50K Landranger or 1:25K Explorer sheets. (Downloaded electronic versions are good, but beware of relying on online-only versions such as Open Street Map or Google Maps, as these require a strong mobile signal, lots of battery power, a clear view of the sky and phone-based satellite GPS.)

- Explorer: sheet 45 covers much of the northern Cotswolds; elsewhere you will need sheets 155, 156, 167, 168, 179, 180, 191 or 205
- Landranger: sheets 151, 163, 164, 172 or 173

Relevant local sheets seem to be becoming less commonly available in local village stores and petrol stations, and are perhaps best bought in advance of a visit.

WAYMARKING AND ACCESS

Gates

Gates abound on entry to/exit from and between fields, particularly on bridleways (rather than byways). I have only mentioned gates where they are vital for navigation, but if you assume there will be a gate at the start and end of every field and across any good downhill off-road trail, you won't go far wrong!

Gates are very common in the Cotswolds – expect to find one at each end of every field and across any nice off-road downhill

Northwick Estate
PRIVATE
Keep to right of way.
Dogs must be
on leads.

Waymarking signs

Many of the routes in this book make use of Sustrans National Cycle Network routes. These are often way-marked with bright blue stickers on lamp posts and other street furniture – places where the signs are easy to spot and harder for bored kids to remove or redirect than conventional fingerposts. They can be very useful, particularly in built-up areas.

Rights of way

Cyclists are permitted on bridleways, restricted byways (no motorised vehicles) and byways (all vehicles allowed).

Bridleways are usually marked with a blue arrow; byways with a 'byway' sign, or sometimes a red arrow; footpaths (which cyclists may not legally ride on) with a yellow arrow. However, it is generally accepted that you can dismount and walk with your bike over a footpath, as is required for a short section of Route 6. Clearly, common sense must also apply: you should not try to push a bike over a narrow single-file foot-path where this would cause inconvenience to walkers.

To confuse the situation, however, there are some footpaths you may ride on. These are typically in urban areas, where many footpaths have become shared pedestrian/cycle path routes (and should be marked with a blue bicycle symbol, sometimes with and sometimes without a pedestrian symbol).

For some other paths the rights are either unclear, lost in time, or (again, particularly in urban areas) in the process of change. They might be commonly used by cycles without landowner opposition, or (occasionally) with landowner encouragement. You should always approach such areas with caution, and if challenged be prepared to dismount or deviate.

Cycle path etiquette
This is particularly important when the route is busy and shared with pedestrians.

- It's fine to go fast if the way is clear, but always slow down to a gentle pace when nearing and passing pedestrians or slower cyclists, or on narrow sections of route.

- Sound your bell as you get close to pedestrians and slower cyclists if you wish to pass them, as this is easiest for other path users to comprehend on a busier route.

- When passing other cycles or pedestrians, use normal road sense: cycle on the **left** when meeting oncoming people, and don't overtake if the way ahead isn't clear!

- Be extremely cautious when cycling under bridges and tunnels – these are often very narrow with restricted headroom at one side, and visibility is often limited.

- Take great care passing dogs (or lone walkers whose dogs may be hidden in the undergrowth), as these can unpredictably change direction or run out in front of

Uphill through Upper Swainswick village (Route 10)

you, sometimes with a long 'trip-wire' lead between them and their owner.

CYCLING EFFICIENTLY

The routes in this book are intended for anyone of average fitness upwards. You do not have to be an athlete by any means, but you will need a basic level of fitness. The following advice may help with hills and off-road sections if you are new to cycling.

Uphill cycling

I regularly see novice (and not-so-novice!) cyclists struggling to push a bike up a steep hill, when just a few simple tips could turn a frustrating slog into a fun challenge (well, OK... perhaps the fun really comes from overcoming the ascent rather than the uphill effort itself). It's so much more enjoyable when you can stay on the bike uphill as well as downhill.

- Use **all** of your lowest gears. That particularly includes those found on the smallest 'hill-climbing' front ring, which so many people ignore. Selecting a low gear in good time and moving gently uphill is far more efficient than standing on the pedals in too high a gear, or going too fast at the start and running out of steam later on.
- Set your saddle to the correct height – too low is a very common mistake for novices, resulting in pain and unnecessary fatigue in the thighs. The saddle should be roughly hip-height and your leg should be almost (but not completely) extended at the bottom of the stroke.
- If there is room and it is safe to do so, use the width of the route to zigzag. This eases the gradient and also helps to relieve monotony.

Off-road cycling

It takes time to get used to off-road riding but the following tips may help those who are new to the fun.

- Initially set the saddle a little lower than usual – this lowers your centre of balance and psychologically feels safer.
- The bike generally heads to the point you are looking at, so look at where you want to go (the route **around** the obstacle, not at the obstacle itself).
- Stay loose, grip the saddle lightly with your thighs, and let your knees and arms act as natural shock absorbers. Allow the bike to move around underneath you; in time you will find you act as a natural counterbalance to it.
- Often a bit of speed helps – but not so much that you couldn't stop or swerve out of the way if something (or someone) is unexpectedly encountered.
- Bike geometry makes a difference and it's worth reading up on this. I personally found a longer-than-usual frame length made a great difference to my off-road

Grassy bridleway near Chavenage House (Route 19)

skills; other people prefer the fast response of a more 'twitchy' shorter-framed bike.

HOW HARD ARE THE ROUTES?

Everyone has different opinions on what makes a route difficult. Some people consider long distance the hardest thing, others the gradient or length of the steepest hill, or maybe the roughness of the surface under-wheel or the use of A-roads. The information boxes at the start of each section in this book help to show the overall difficulty of individual routes.

Terrain

The terrain statistics shown in the information boxes at the start of each route give some clue as to the amount of off-road involved.

'Trails' are purpose-made traffic-free cycle routes, such as Sustrans-style routes. Such sections tend to be gently graded with a smooth, firm (gravel or tarmac) surface.

'Off-road' is any other non-road (or sometimes a former road) section, which may be steeper, rougher and muddier – or just an unclassified bit of road. In technical terms, it's a middle ground between 'out and back' totally car-free cycling and that which more properly falls into technical mountain biking. Hybrid bikes (often referred to as 'sturdy' bikes, although this term includes any road bike that isn't too narrow-tyred or fragile to be taken off-road) should usually manage most off-road routes in dry conditions, except for rough sections. Most of these are highlighted in the route description, but remember that the condition of

25

the ground is variable depending on prevailing weather conditions. Also see additional notes in the information box at the start of each route.

The routes use many of the region's quiet lanes, bridleways, byways and ancient paths. You will need traffic sense as the routes do use public roads, but most are suitable for families with older children who have mastered the rules of the road sufficiently to be safe in traffic.

Grades

For the purpose of this guidebook I've graded the routes Easy, Moderate or Challenging according to the following criteria. However, while the harder routes tend to include more challenges, the terrain statistics show that the easy routes aren't devoid of them!

'Easy' routes are relatively short (less than 25km), not overly steep and should not climb one hill after another (cumulative ascent no more than 300m). They only travel along A-roads for very short sections in urban centres (although they may well have to cross them, and other minor roads can be surprisingly busy). They will not usually have much off-road terrain; any off-road tends to be easier than that found on harder routes, but short sections may seem unrideable if you have limited experience of off-road cycling.

'Moderate' routes can be longer (14km to 45km), have steeper ascents and more hills in general (cumulative ascent no more than 500m); they may also have very steep downhills. They may tackle short sections of A-road (sometimes outside of urban

Descending on the bridleway near Berryfields Farm

Everyone has their own opinion on what makes a route hard – here the off-road climb is tough but short (Route 2)

areas) where needed to join up parts of a good circular route, and may encounter rougher terrain on a more frequent basis or for a longer duration (eg lumpy but solid surfaces, mud and loose stones). These more challenging sections will never last too long, but again, short sections may seem unrideable if you have limited experience of off-road cycling.

'Challenging' routes may feel noticeably harder than the other routes in the book. They are the longer routes (35km to 60km) and typically have more than 500m of cumulative ascent. Although they're likely to include short sections of technical mountain biking (Routes 21 and 17 in particular), they are never out-and-out technical off-road routes. However, they may contain short sections that many riders will consider unrideable on an otherwise great route.

Day route vs multi-day route

Although no stage in Route 22 is tougher than a 'challenging' route, riders should not underestimate the cumulative effect of fatigue on a multi-day outing. On the other hand, its relatively few off-road sections are optional and it is well suited to all types of bike. Keen, fit and experienced riders, particularly those on road bikes, may well wish to compress this route into a two- or three-day challenge.

Wet conditions

After prolonged rain (and often in winter) many routes change character completely from their hard-baked summer surface. Woodland bridleways in particular are notoriously slow to dry. Some route descriptions give suggestions for on-road detours to avoid more awkward off-road sections; it is recommended that you use an OS map in conjunction with these. A few of the routes may be simply impractical in very wet conditions due to the amount and state of the off-road. On all surfaces, remember that braking distances should be considerably extended in the wet.

USING THIS GUIDE

This guide describes 21 day routes and one multi-day route, arranged roughly in order of difficulty from easy through to challenging. To find a route to suit your location and your ability, check the table in Appendix A. Timings are not given for routes because the variation between those who like to amble along enjoying the scenery and those who want to do the route with head down and flat out is simply too great. Also, your speed on any given route or day will vary based a whole variety of things such as terrain, poor weather (including it being too hot or facing a headwind) and fatigue.

As a vague rule of thumb, the day routes in this book are designed to occupy from a fairly leisurely half day (easier/shorter routes) to a full day (moderate/challenging, longer or particularly off-road routes), with stops for refreshments.

At-a-glance information is provided in a box at the beginning of each route: start/finish (OS map reference and place name); distance; total ascent and descent; grade; terrain (percentages of road/trail/off-road); refreshment, parking and cycle hire options; suitability for road bikes; details of connecting routes; and any

The bridleway between Aston Somerville and Childswickham (Route 5)

additional notes relevant to the route. Route 22 (multi-day) also includes accommodation options. Clear route maps at 1:100,000 (1cm to 1km) and also simple profiles accompany each route description and GPX files are available for every route at www. cicerone.co.uk/CyclingCotswolds. See the back of this guide for full details.

Staying on-road

Where the main route described goes off-road, an **on-road** alternative is described in the margin and marked on the map with a dashed route line.

Warnings

Warnings, including comments about tricky terrain, are also highlighted in the margin on coloured panels to make them hard to miss.

Conventions and abbreviations

Routes on the Sustrans National Cycle Network are abbreviated to NCN followed by the route number, for example National Cycle Network Route 5 is NCN5. Long-distance cycle routes, such as the Avon Cycle Way, are also abbreviated to their acronyms (ACW).

'Towards' or 'to'

Where a signpost or map direction takes you towards a place (such as Bibury), but you will turn off before getting there, it is described as '**towards** Bibury'. Where it takes you all the way there, it is written as '**to** Bibury'.

Key waypoints

Places and features are highlighted in bold in the route description if they are shown on the accompanying route map, giving you an at-a-glance checklist of key waypoints. OS Grid references are given in a few places where there is no other suitable landmark/map feature available.

Turnings and junctions

Generally, 'bend' is used to describe the course of the road, not a junction. For junctions, 'bear' or 'fork' means a deviation of noticeably less than 90°, whereas 'turn' means roughly 90° and a 'sharp turn' is more than 90°. 'Dog-leg' is used to describe a turn (with or without a junction) one way, closely followed by a turn in the opposite direction, to end up on roughly the original course.

Side-turns, minor, major and main roads and crossroads

In keeping with Bikeability conventions, this guidebook sometimes makes use of the terms 'minor road' and 'major road'. These terms do not give any indication of size or traffic volume, but refer to the priority of traffic at a junction, with traffic (which includes bicycles) on a minor road having to give way to traffic on the major road.

Priorities are only mentioned where it is useful for navigational purposes or where they are deemed essential (for example a minor road meeting a major road on a steep

Sunset over the scarp edge looking down towards Winchcombe

descent or round a blind bend), but everybody will have a different opinion as to which priorities are important and which aren't. It's also worth bearing in mind that road layouts change over time.

I've also extended the terms to crossroads, so a 'minor crossroads' is one where you are on the major road and are crossing over minor roads, and a 'major crossroads' is one where you are on the minor road and have to give way to the major road.

A 'main road' is usually an A-road. I try to avoid these as much as possible, but the Cotswolds are riddled with them, and crossing over them, or using them for very short

sections, is often unavoidable. In such cases these sections are kept as short as possible, and are ideally in areas of lower speed limits (for example within villages) or on a downhill stretch. There will, of course, always be the occasional exception to this – for example within Bath City Centre (Route 6).

Should you come across a junction that isn't mentioned (these tend to be insignificant side-turns or a series of minor roads crossing over the major road in a short space of time), just remember the route will always take the major road (and usually continue straight ahead) if no other mention is made.

ROUTE 1

Shipston-on-Stour Loop via Brailes Hill

Start/Finish	The White Bear Inn, Shipston-on-Stour (SP 258 405)
Distance	23km (14 miles)
Total ascent/descent	260m
Grade	Easy
Terrain	100% roads
Refreshments	On route: The George Inn (Lower Brailes); La Tradition Bakery (Upper Brailes); The Gate Inn (Upper Brailes); White Bear Inn (Shipston) Short detour: Cherington Arms PH (Cherington); various in Shipston
Parking	Car parks in Shipston (free)
Cycle hire	Chipping Campden or TY Cycles (mobile)
Road bikes?	Yes
Connecting routes	Route 2

This is a fairly gentle introduction to the rolling Cotswold hills. Sibford Lane feels steep, but is short in reality, with good views. There's a choice of pubs and even a French bakery en-route.

Head S from the pub, then turn left onto the one-way West Street (a small gyratory system), following NCN5 signs. ▸ Give way to incoming traffic from your right and use the right-hand lane at the next junction. Take the next left off the gyratory onto Mill Street (B4035) towards Brailes. Continue over a narrow bridge and gently uphill. Where the road bends left, turn right to **Barcheston**. As soon as you leave the B4035 you feel out in the quiet countryside, with good views, particularly of Brailes Hill on the left.

Turn right at a triangular T-junction and continue past the edge of **Willington**, initially heading towards Burmington and then towards Cherington. The road now rises steadily uphill to reach an incoming track just past **Burmington Grange**.

Turn right here and descend gently to a T-junction roughly 500m later. Turn left (effectively continuing

You can follow these signs all the way past Sutton-under-Brailes.

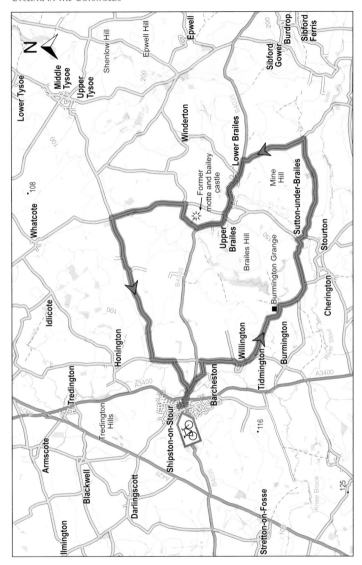

straight ahead) towards Cherington.
Take the next left to **Sutton-under-Brailes**, roughly contouring to the
village. Bend right then left past
a church and pass a large village
green. Turn right just beyond this
and descend towards Stourton.

Take the next left towards
Sibford. This takes you around Mine
Hill on the way to Brailes Hill.

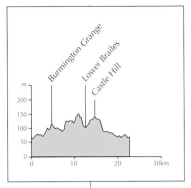

Brailes Hill is one of the highest
hills in the region, and at 232m
is less than 30m lower than
Ebrington Hill near Ilmington (the highest point
in Warwickshire). It is the main hill that the route
circumnavigates.

The road continues for roughly 2.5km before reaching the next junction. It rises, initially, for 600m on a sustained uphill. In reality you are barely gaining 50m – it

*The valley just north
of Upper Brailes is
surprisingly flat*

just feels like a lot more! That said, the views to the right once you've gained some height are well worth the effort. It then levels out before descending past a sharp bend left to a T-junction.

Turn left towards Brailes and climb gently over another rounded shoulder of Mine Hill before descending, 1.8km later, to a road on the edge of **Lower Brailes**. Turn left here and enjoy the descent into the village, passing The George PH as the gradient levels. Now head uphill, staying on the major road and passing an excellent (if unexpected) French bakery on your left as you come into **Upper Brailes**. The road now rises, passing The Gate PH.

Roughly 400m beyond this, turn right onto Castle Hill. ◀

> A former **motte and bailey castle** once stood proud above Upper Brailes. Only earthworks and buried remnants still exist, but it is thought the castle was built on a natural knoll, which was raised further by the Normans to form the 'motte' of the motte and bailey.

This road gently rises to a sharp right-hand bend and then descends gently towards a T-junction. Immediately before this junction, turn left onto a minor road towards Whatcote.

Enjoy a fantastic descent to a crossroads and turn left towards Honington. Continue descending very gently for nearly 4km further to a T-junction. Turn left towards Barcheston and rise gently uphill. Pass the entrance to a sewage works and then turn right onto a minor road. Rise initially and then descend gently to a T-junction on the edge of **Shipston-on-Stour**. Turn right and continue over the narrow bridge.

Continue past a car park to reach a junction with the one-way system. Give way to traffic on the right – there is a cycle lane to help you. Turn right onto New Street, and a dog-leg left then right takes you back to your start point.

This is both easily missed and potentially dangerous; make sure you continue past the former spring to take the one-way entry lane to this road.

ROUTE 2

Shipston-on-Stour Loop via Halford

Start/Finish	The White Bear Inn, Shipston-on-Stour (SP 258 405)
Distance	24km (15 miles)
Total ascent/descent	255m
Grade	Easy
Terrain	81% roads, 19% off-road
Refreshments	On route: several in Shipston; Farm Shop Bakery (Talton Mill) Short detour: The Halford PH
Parking	Car parks in Shipston (free)
Cycle hire	Chipping Campden or TY Cycles (mobile)
Road bikes?	Will require two detours to avoid off-road sections – the first via Ilmington, the second involving short sections of major roads (A3400 and A429) through Newbold to Halford.
Connecting routes	Routes 1 and 11
Note	Includes one section of bridleway that may be challenging for those new to off-road riding, but it is very short and provides an alternative to busy A-roads, so is worth persevering with.

This is a lovely route in classic Cotswolds territory with some attractive bridleways through fields. The only potentially awkward section of off-road is short-lived, and the A-road crossing between Crimscote and Ettington is straightforward. The historic pub at Halford is within spitting distance of the route partway round.

Head S from the pub, then turn right onto West Street (a two-way road here). Rise uphill then turn right towards Ilmington on Darlingscott Road, rising moderately steeply past a school and out of town (following NCN5).

Cross the A429 and continue along a wide but twisty lane to

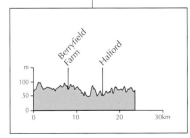

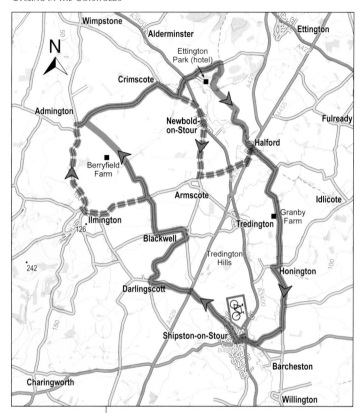

Darlingscott. In the village, turn right to Blackwell (now leaving NCN5), bending right past some pretty, old buildings.

After roughly 1.6km turn left towards Ilmington at an unusual junction from one minor road to another. Turn left at a crossroads, and left again at an oblique junction opposite **Blackwell Grange** (a thatched roof barn in some disrepair). ◄

Once out of the village, take a minor road to the right. Shortly after a sharp bend left, cross a road, taking

This barn may well be redeveloped in the lifetime of this guidebook – at the time of writing a planning application had been submitted to build a wedding venue in its place.

36

a dead-end lane towards **Berryfield Farm**. ▸ This lane twists and turns until you reach the farm driveway on a left-hand bend. Continue straight ahead along a dirt/grassy track for roughly 1.5km. The track rises up beside fields to pass near a large barn before descending to a country lane.

Turn right here and undulate gently through Crimscote Fields to reach the main village of **Crimscote**, some distance after the village sign. Bend sharp right and go up a short but steep hill. Bend left past a large estate (Talton House) and keep following iron railings round to the left at a triangular grassy junction. ▸ Continue past a farm shop to reach the A3400. Dog-leg left then right over this road towards Ettington village. (Don't go straight ahead – it's a hotel driveway.)

Ettington holds claim to fame as the village with the longest connection to one single family, with the Shirleys having owned the manor since at least 1086 (they appear in the Domesday Book). The current Ettington Manor (now the hotel whose

To stay **on road**, turn left here to Ilmington (see dashed line on map) and then follow signs to Admington and Crimscote.

To stay **on road**, carry straight on here to Newbold-on-Stour (see dashed line on map) and then follow signs to Armscote and Halford.

The quiet country lane junction opposite Blackwell Grange

driveway you've just passed) is thought to stand near the site of a Roman villa, and is reputed to be haunted. Local legend also claims that William Shakespeare often stayed here while hunting with the Shirleys.

Continue past Ettington Business Park and through a wooded area towards the top of the hill. As the road begins to descend turn right onto a bridleway, descending on a wide vehicle track. ◄ At a clearing, bend right then left and enjoy a continuing descent on a reasonable vehicle track. This fades somewhat after a dip; continue straight ahead through the fields, heading between two sets of oak trees to a slight summit.

This off-road section continues for just over 2.5km to Halford village.

Shortly after this, cross a faint field boundary and descend rightwards. An awkward rut appears on the descent; this section to the bottom of the dip may prove challenging, even in dry conditions, to those new to off-road riding. ◄ You may have to fight, very briefly, through the sometimes-overgrown vegetation in the bottom of the dip; the way then eases as you rise back to the general field level. Once up this rise, bend left, following the edge of fields. (Do not go straight ahead to descend steeply towards the river.)

Should you need to dismount, don't despair – this doesn't last at all long!

Eventually the path splits; bear left and go through a small wooden gate. Bear diagonally right across this grassy meadow, aiming just right of building roofs until you can see a small gate. Go through this and over a bridge across a small stream, now heading just right of a thin shrubby hedge.

Pass through a gate to the left of a white house and turn right onto a residential road in **Halford**.

Halford has been a major crossing point on the Fosse Way over the River Stour since Roman times. Some sources say the name was originally Aldford – as in 'old ford' – suggesting its ancient origins as a Roman fording point. The pub here, now called The Halford, dates from the 16th century, presumably as a staging post for travellers along the Fosse Way.

Continue past the church then go left at the next junction to reach a major road (A429). Cross this into Idlicote Road. Where the road bends sharp left, turn right onto a minor (gated) road to **Granby**. Stay on this road past an old rusty windmill to reach the edge of **Honington village**.

The bridleway to Halford runs between a couple of pairs of oaks

Turn right at the T-junction towards Shipston, then take the next left towards Barcheston (by a small green with a very old 'Best kept village' wooden sign). Ignore a minor road to the left and rise gently uphill. Pass the entrance to a sewage works and then turn right onto a minor road.

Rise initially, then descend gently to a T-junction on the edge of **Shipston**. Turn right and continue over the narrow bridge. Continue past a car park to reach the one-way system. Give way to traffic on the right – there is a cycle lane to help you. Turn right onto New Street, and a dog-leg left then right takes you back to your start point.

ROUTE 3
Shipton-under-Wychwood Loop via Wychwood

Start/Finish	Shaven Crown Hotel, Shipton-under-Wychwood (SP 278 178)
Distance	22km (14 miles)
Total ascent/descent	270m
Grade	Easy
Terrain	82% roads, 18% off-road
Refreshments	On route: Shaven Crown Hotel (Shipton); Swan Inn (Ascott-under-Wychwood)Short detour: The Navy Oak and Fox Inn (Leafield); Café de la Post (Chadlington); Lamb Inn (Shipton)
Parking	Very limited (on road) in Shipton
Cycle hire	Bourton-on-the-Water or TY Cycles (mobile)
Road bikes?	Detour using B4437 to avoid the bridleway east of Ascott
Connecting routes	Route 9
Note	Shipton and Ascott rail stations have such a limited service that they almost don't exist on the railway timetable.

Another gentle introduction to some of the best things about riding in the Cotswolds: quiet lanes, gentle bridleways beside streams, and a few hills to add to the challenge (these are not too steep, although the ascent at Wychwood Forest may seem quite long).

If you wish to stay **on road**, turn right here with the main road (see dashed line on map) and then follow signs to Chilson, turning right to Leafield to rejoin the main route.

Take the minor road towards **Ascott-under-Wychwood**. This soon bends sharp right at a junction; take the minor road left. ◄ Stay on this road, bending right by Ascott Earl House. Continue through the village, passing the Swan Inn, and turn left over a level crossing.

Just past the bridge over the River Evenlode, bear right through a small gate onto the Oxfordshire Way bridleway (not waymarked). A Coldstone AC sign aids visibility, particularly in summer. Briefly fight through vegetation to reach the edge of a large field that roughly follows beside the river. Ignore a bridge over the river and stay to the right-hand side of two large fields to reach a corner.

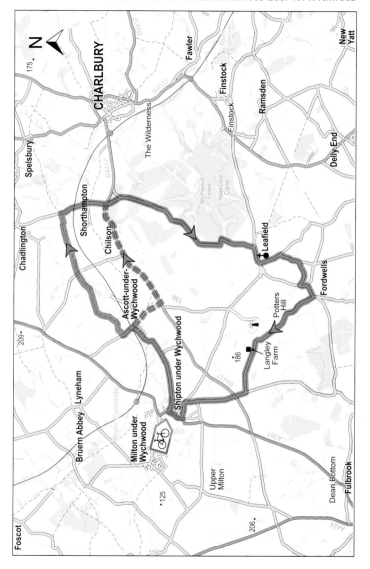

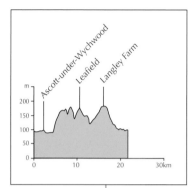

The path goes through a gate and crosses a tiny stream on a slabby bridge before continuing on the left side of the field. Continue ahead in the next field, going straight across the middle of a grassy meadow on a faint path, heading just right of a garage-like structure. Then follow the left edge of the next field and go along a line of trees and wooden posts to reach a vehicle track. Continue along this and cross a country lane.

Now follow the clearly-way-marked bridleway almost directly straight ahead and along the left edge of fields for roughly 1.5km, dodging briefly right then left to cross a small concrete bridge over a stream towards the end. Turn right onto a country lane and rise steadily uphill for roughly 1.4km to reach a slightly staggered crossroads. Dog-leg right then left over this, then head right at the next T-junction.

Riding up the hill towards Wychwood Forest

This lane rises gently over the next 4.5km, but undulates significantly along the way, and dips in and out of the woodland of Wychwood Forest.

In Norman times **Wychwood Forest** extended across much of the region now known as the Cotswolds. In those days 'forest' simply meant an area of reserved hunting rights (usually for the local noblemen) – wooded or not. However, the woodland is now recognised as ancient broadleaved woodland, and is known to have existed at the time of the Domesday book (1086).

The name Wychwood is thought to have even older origins: from a tribe called the Hwicce (whose name is possibly itself derived from the Angle Gewisse groups that arrived in the area in the late 6th century). Alternatively, 'wych' (or wich) sometimes means a salt well – as in Droitwich or Middlewich further north.

A sharp bend left (with tracks heading off right) marks a high point; descend from this to a dip by a forestry entrance, then rise steadily again to the edge of **Leafield**. Turn right here towards Shipton-under-Wychwood and rise gently through the village. Turn left immediately after the church, onto Witney Lane. Enjoy the descent and then stay on the major road as it bends right towards Minster Lovell.

Roughly 600m later take a minor road right (Purrants Lane). ▶ At the end, turn left opposite a tennis court and then, as the road begins to rise more steeply, fork right towards **Fordwells**. ▶

On the edge of Fordwells turn right at a T-junction towards Shipton. This lane rises for roughly 2.5km, feeling steepest near **Langley Farm**. ▶ At the end, turn right and continue straight ahead over a major crossroads.

This descends to the edge of **Shipton**, ending at a complicated five-way junction. Stay left (on another minor road, signposted to Shipton with weight limit). Descend to reach a main road (A361). Turn right onto this and descend gently back to the start.

This is easily missed – look for a stone building on a bend.

Caution when turning right – blind bend.

The climb is worthwhile: once back on the plateau there are good views right across the vale.

ROUTE 4

Bourton-on-the-Water Loop via the Slaughters

Start/Finish	War memorial, village green, Bourton-on-the-Water (SP 168 207)
Distance	23km (14 miles)
Total ascent/descent	300m
Grade	Easy
Terrain	61% roads, 39% off-road
Refreshments	On route: several in Bourton; Black Horse Inn (Naunton); The Slaughters Inn (Lower Slaughter) Short detour: Farmers Arms (Guiting Power); Golden Ball Inn (Lower Swell)
Parking	Village car parks, Bourton (fee)
Cycle hire	Bourton or TY Cycles (mobile)
Road bikes?	Yes, but with several detours. These are short near Naunton and the Slaughters. The detour via Lower Swell is rather longer. The Eyford Park track is reasonable for sturdy road bikes (hybrids, for example) but the bridleways from Bourton and Wyck Rissington are rather rough. Road cyclists should follow route description for Route 22, Day 3 from Upper Slaughter to Bourton to avoid the latter.
Connecting routes	Routes 7 and 17
Note	Do not be tempted to avoid the hill (near Hill Farm) by the continuation bridleway running on the southwest bank of the River Windrush unless you are a confident mountain biker – it has very steep gradients and can be quite rough in places.

Overall this is a relatively gentle route, but it has a couple of steep hills early on (the rise from Naunton village seems particularly steep). The rewards include sneaking away from the honeypot town of Bourton-on-the-Water on some lovely sections of bridleway, and the high track through Eyford Park. The picture-postcard villages of Upper and Lower Slaughter, and a few challenges along the way (an optional easy ford crossing and a short section of bridleway that looks a lot harder than it really is), make for added interest.

Head NW out of town on the High Street (immediately passing a prominent fish and chip shop on your left) to

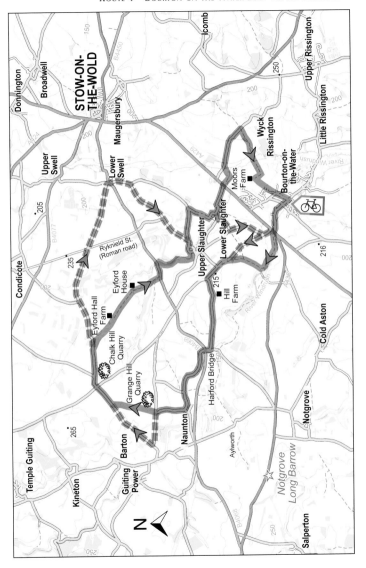

The bridleway parallel to the River Windrush near Bourton-on-the-Water

To stay **on road**, take the minor road setting off north west from the A429 (see map).

The next section looks more intimidating than it really is.

Take this steady and gentle.

Be vigilant at the bottom of this lane as you join another minor road almost immediately on the junction with the B4068.

reach a junction with a main road (A429). Cross this to gain a bridleway (the Windrush Way) through a gate opposite. ◄ This runs along a dirt/grassy track (initially fenced on both sides) beside a hay meadow. Continue through a second field, which narrows towards its end.

◄ Immediately through a gate, bend right and go steeply uphill, then fork right at a wooden bridleway markerpost. Go over an awkward-looking vague remnant of drystone wall (also much easier than it looks!). An easier-going trail now leads to a descent. ◄ Exit the wood and reach a junction of tracks. Turn right, following bridleway waymarkers (the Gloucester Way), and go up a wide but fairly steep track. This bends left and then joins a minor road.

Turn left onto this and ignore a side-turn right to the Slaughters. Just past Colne Saddlery, at a sharp bend right, turn left to Lower Harford. This contours then descends, increasingly steeply, from Harford House to **Harford Bridge**. ◄ Cross the B4068 and continue to **Naunton**, running parallel with the River Windrush after an initial brief ascent.

In the village, ignore the first turn right (just after the pub) and a dead-end lane, and shortly after a red phone box take the next right (by a house called Windrush Vale) going steeply uphill to a junction by Grange Hill Quarry. Continue straight across this onto a byway, initially running along the steep driveway entrance to the quarry. ▸ Where quarry traffic turns off right, continue ahead and keep going along a surprisingly nice track between fields for roughly 1.2km. Descend gently to a country lane, turn right onto this and go straight across the next junction with a major road.

Continue along this road for roughly 1.2km then bear right onto a bridleway running along a tarmac driveway to **Eyford Hill Farm**. ▸ Continue past the farm and through Eyford Park to a T-junction with a major road (roughly 2.6km of track).

> The grounds of **Eyford House** are said to have been the inspiration for John Milton to start writing Paradise Lost while he was staying there in 1658. Sadly little is visible of the grounds from the rights of way, but the views over the Upper Dikler Valley from the upper end of the track are rather pleasant.

Turn left and go gently downhill towards a bridge over a stream. Just before the bridge, turn right onto a bridleway track (Warden's Way) running beside the stream, and continue into the pretty village of **Upper Slaughter**. Turn left and go through the ford (or over the bridge if it's running too high). The lane then bends right and continues to reach a more major lane. Turn left along this and bend sharp left, then fork right towards Lower Slaughter.

To stay **on road**, head left then right (see map) to join the country lane north of the quarry.

To stay **on road**, stay on the road to Lower Swell (see map) and follow signs to Upper Slaughter.

47

Crossing the ford at Upper Slaughter

To stay **on road**, continue south on minor roads through the village (see map) finally turning left across the Fosse Way (A429) to return to Bourton-on-the-Water.

The name **Slaughter** has nothing to do with past violent battles but is instead derived from the Old English word 'slohtre', which means a muddy place, ditch or muddy ford.

At an oblique T-junction, turn sharp right and descend into **Lower Slaughter**. ◄ Continue on the major road, bending left, right, and left again past the church and The Slaughters Country Inn. Continue following this to a T-junction with the Fosse Way (A429). Cross this, taking a bridleway opposite. This bends sharp left after 300m, then a further 300m later it joins a country lane. Turn right along this and follow it into the hamlet of **Wyck Rissington**.

Turn right opposite a postbox onto a bridleway. Continue over rough ground in the first couple of fields, bending right towards the end of the second to reach a pair of small wooden gates on either side of a sleeper bridge. ◄ The ground is now much easier-going.

Do not go through the more visible large metal gate.

◄ Continue over two further sleeper bridges and through gates to reach a dirt track. Turn right along this, then left onto a stone track at the end. Turn left at the end of the track onto a residential road, and very quickly left again onto a main road. Where this bends sharp left, turn right into Bourton's High Street. Continue up here to return to the start.

Here you are passing through Greystones Farm Nature Reserve, where the land has been farmed for more than 6000 years.

ROUTE 5

Alderton via Broadway

Start/Finish	Gardeners Arms PH, Alderton (SP 000 333)
Alternative start	West end of Broadway, opposite Childswickham Road (SP 091 376)
Distance	35km (22 miles)
Total ascent/descent	215m
Grade	Moderate
Terrain	93% roads, 3% trail, 4% off-road
Refreshments	On route: Gardeners Arms PH (Alderton); Beckford Inn, Silk Museum Café (Beckford); Picturesque Café (Dumbleton); plenty in Broadway Short detour: Childswickham Inn
Parking	Limited parking on road in Alderton
Cycle hire	Chipping Campden, Cheltenham, Moreton-in-Marsh, Stratford or TY Cycles (mobile)
Road bikes?	Off-road near Childswickham unsuitable for road bikes – suggested detour via Buckland Fields.
Connecting routes	Route 22
Note	The OS Explorer 1:25K map differs from several other maps in the location of the end of the bridleway near Childswickham, but it shows the correct version (as described here). Roads going under the disused railway near Wormington/Laverton can flood deeply – a suggested detour would continue along B4632 and take the following right past Wormington Grange.

This is a good route for those who like seeing hills without the effort of climbing them, although it does involve some B-roads. It also visits Broadway – one of the most popular villages in the Cotswolds.

Head W from the Gardeners Arms, turning right almost immediately to Beckford. Stay on the major road as you pass the tiny hamlet of **Great Washbourne**, and take a dog-leg left then right over the busy **A46** into Station Road, passing the Beckford Inn on your left. At a sharp

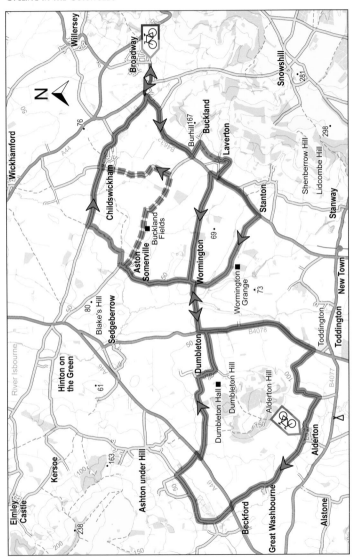

bend left in **Beckford**, turn right towards Grafton on Ashton Road. Pass the Silk Museum and turn right at a minor cross-roads towards Evesham.

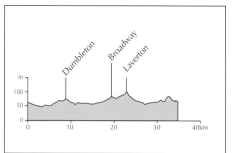

This road leads again to the **A46**. Turn right onto the main road, then after 150m go left onto a country lane to **Dumbleton**. This now takes you around the N side of Dumbleton Hill and, at the end of the village, past the entrance to Dumbleton Hall. ▸

Bend left here and descend gently to a major road (B4078). Turn left towards Sedgebarrow and then take the next right (unsigned, to **Wormington**). In the village, bend left then take a minor road left (effectively continuing straight ahead) to **Aston Somerville**. Ignore a minor road right towards Broadway in the village, instead taking the next right (by a red phone box on a sharp bend

This is nowadays a hotel, but local legend has it that if Hitler had conquered Britain this was the place he wanted to use as his personal residence.

Dumbleton has several typical Cotswolds buildings – here a honey-coloured limestone house sits next to a half-timbered one

To stay **on road**, take the minor right right towards Broadway (see map) and take the next left turn to Childswickham.

left). ◄ This soon becomes a bridleway track leading into a field. Turn left at the field entrance and follow the left edge of the field past a narrowing by a white pole. Continue through a second field to reach an open boundary between fields. Bend slightly right then left here, still heading roughly NE, now running beside a dyke at the right-hand side of this field. Near the end of this field the bridleway bears right over a tiny bridge then exits onto a wide road.

> Evesham Vale is renowned for its orchards, and in spring (mid-March to mid-May), those along this road form part of the **Spring Blossom Trail** – a 45-mile route celebrating the beautiful blossom of the fruit trees dotted throughout the region.

The Upper High Street of Broadway is less busy and has many fine examples of older buildings built of golden limestone

Turn right along this and continue through **Childswickham** to the end of the road on the edge of **Broadway**. Detour briefly into Broadway (follow signs to the village centre) before returning to this point, now continuing SW on the B4632 for roughly 2km towards Buckland.

*Cyclist descending the former road from Naunton Farm.
Once beyond this farm, the tarmac deteriorates noticeably*

Turn left to **Buckland** at a minor crossroads and continue to a red phone box on a slight left-hand bend. Turn
around and you will now see a bridleway heading off
left (at about 11 o'clock). Follow this Sustrans-style path
to **Laverton**; as you reach the village, turn right then left
onto a country lane. Follow this to a T-junction and turn
left then right onto the B4632. ▶

Take the next left towards **Wormington**, bending left
then right through the hamlet. Turn left at a T-junction
onto the B4078 and follow this for roughly 3.5km.
Shortly after a fencing supplies business on the left, and
an agricultural suppliers on the right, take a small minor
lane rightwards (not signposted).

Follow this gently uphill for roughly 700m to a sharp
bend right and then turn left onto a deteriorated tarmac track (a former road that is no longer maintained).
Continue along this, bending left towards the farmhouse
ahead where two footpaths branch off right. Bend right
then left by the farmhouse and descend to a road junction. Turn right along this, staying on the major road to
return to Alderton.

After heavy rain it
may be better to turn
left here (see map)
to avoid possible
flooding.

ROUTE 6

Bradford on Avon via Bath Two Tunnels

Start/Finish	Canal Tavern, Bradford on Avon (ST 826 603)
Distance	34km (21 miles)
Total ascent/descent	315m
Grade	Mixed: easy trails and challenging city-centre roads
Terrain	13% roads, 87% trails
Refreshments	On route: Lock-in Café/Canalside Tavern (Bradford); Cross Guns PH (Avoncliff); Angelfish Café/Wheelwright Arms PH (Monkton Combe); Golden Fleece PH (Bath – A36); The George Inn (Bathampton) Short detour: Mad Hatter Café (Avoncliff); Hope and Anchor PH (Midford); large choice in Bath (riverside/centre)
Parking	Car park at the end of Bailey's Barn, Bradford on Avon (fee)
Cycle hire	Bath, Bradford on Avon, Bristol or Chippenham (Lacock)
Road bikes?	Yes, if tyres can cope with towpaths
Connecting routes	Route 10
Notes	Two sets of gates – at the end of Brassknocker Basin and onto the road to the sports centre – are locked at night, making the route impassable after 9.00pm in summer and 6.00pm in winter. Navigationally the sections along the canal towpath and through the tunnels are very easy, so only the key navigation points will be described there. It is worth noting that the canal bridges are numbered in decreasing order from Bath to Bradford.

This would be the gentlest route in the book were it not for Bath City Centre, where it briefly falls onto busy roads. Otherwise it runs along easy canal towpaths, a brand new Sustrans trail and the Bath riverside path, making a gentle day out.

If unused to busy city cycling, short sections of this route (in Bath City Centre) could be very challenging despite the route's easy grade.

Head W between the Lock Inn Café and the Canal Tavern and go along the canal towpath. Immediately before the Avoncliff aqueduct, by the Cross Guns PH, the path

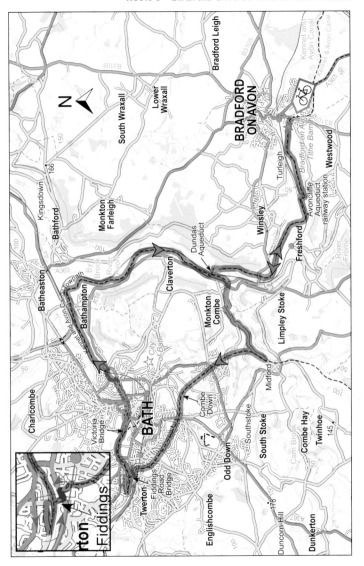

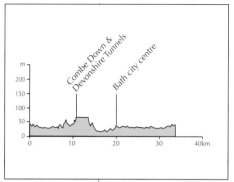

Combe Down & Devonshire Tunnels

Bath city centre

swaps to the left bank via an underpass (follow NCN4 signs).

The idea of a canal linking Bristol with London was first suggested in the late 15th century as an alternative to coastal transport (which was dangerous due to stormy seas and French privateers/warships), but it was 1810 before the **Kennet and Avon Canal** became a reality. Its heyday lasted three decades; the Great Western Railway (GWR) then acquired the canal and promptly made it economically unattractive in comparison to its new railway. Restoration in the late 1990s has allowed it to reopen as a leisure route.

Houseboats are a common sight along the Kennet and Avon Canal

Cross the aqueduct and continue on the left bank to the Dundas aqueduct (roughly 4km). ▸

Immediately after the aqueduct turn left onto a cycle path (now following NCN24). This initially runs alongside the Brassknocker Basin, then bends left and goes downhill to a car park. Continue through gates at the end; turn right onto a narrow lane and go under a road bridge. At **Monkton Combe** Sports Centre turn right into the car park, then head right and uphill to reach a short pavement section between buildings. Dismount for this (it's extremely steep) and continue past a small car park.

At the top, turn left onto Church Lane. Pass the school and Wheelwright's Arms, continuing uphill as the road bends right then left near the church. Turn left onto Tucking Mill Lane, descending steeply at first. Continue for roughly 1.5km, passing the mill in a dip.

At a widening in the wooded lane turn right through a narrow gateway and right again onto the Two Tunnels Greenway (TTG, NCN244). Follow this shared use path for roughly 6km, passing through the Combe Down and Devonshire tunnels and along Linear Park.

This was the first canal structure to be designated a Scheduled Ancient Monument (in 1951).

Entrance to the Combe Down tunnel

The **Two Tunnels Greenway** section of route was opened in April 2013 after significant local fund-raising, much of which was generated from the sale of King Bladud's Pigs. These sculptures commemorated the local legend that Bath was founded when the discovery of leprosy-curing mud enabled Prince Bladud (then living as an outcast leprous swineherd) to return to society and become King of Britain. The Combe Down tunnel, at 1670m long, is claimed by Sustrans to be the longest tunnel in Europe on a cycle route.

At the end of the path, bend right then left onto a residential road, following 'Bath and Bristol via riverside path'. ◄

Cross a railway bridge on a short section of one-way road. Following signs for TTG/NCN244 towards the riverside path, a short cycle path leads to the dead-end of a residential road (Inverness Road). At a T-junction turn right onto Burnham Road. Turn left and briefly onto the A36. ◄

Turn right onto Fieldings Road just in front of the Golden Fleece PH. As the road narrows, dismount to cross a pedestrian footbridge over the river (it's a footpath only). Where this pavement joins a road, remount and turn right, bend almost immediately left, and then go left at a crossroads onto Locksbrook Road (one-way). Continue ahead as this bends left past the Dolphin PH, then bend sharp left, almost going back on yourself, and onto the riverside path heading to Bath City Centre (you should now be able to follow NCN4 signs all the way to Bradford). ◄ Continue straight ahead for roughly 1.5km, taking particular care at narrow sections of path.

Shortly after Victoria Bridge, fork left onto a residential lane with a green to your right. Continue straight ahead into a road marked 'No Entry (Except Cycles)'; go across the next crossroads and over a short section of cycle path to reach a main road.

Cross this via a toucan crossing and continue uphill on a pavement cycle path. Another toucan crossing takes

Sustrans suggest this will change in early 2014, with the Linear Park route being extended over a former railway bridge, thus avoiding the one-way bridge that currently comes next.

The footpath beside this road may gain a cycle path in 2014.

It may be that a right of way for cyclists, leading directly from the bridge onto the riverside path, will be sorted in the lifetime of the current edition of this guide. Check the Cicerone website for updates.

you across Monmouth Street, then head right on a dedicated cycle path. This bends left around The Griffin Inn and crosses into Beauford Square. Continue through bollards and go right onto Barton Street. Go through more bollards by Molloy's PH and bear left. ▸

At a T-junction, turn right onto Walcot Street, bending left onto Bridge Street. Stay left to go straight ahead onto Pulteney Bridge, where most other traffic has to turn right. Give way to traffic as Grove Street joins from the left and continue over Laura Place. ▸ Continue to the end of Great Pulteney Street.

> The Laura Place **fountain** is a much shorter replacement for the 'Nelson's Column' that the residents of Great Pulteney Street commissioned in the late 18th century – which they rejected when they realised it would be significantly taller than their own houses.

Turn left onto the very busy A36 towards Warminster. Get into the right-hand lane as soon as possible to filter right at the traffic lights. Bend sharp right (the road then rises steeply uphill) and go across a (not very obvious) bridge. Immediately after this turn left onto the canal towpath. Head E to **Bathhampton**. The route now stays on the canal towpath for roughly 14km back to Bradford-on-Avon.

Pass the George PH after roughly 2.2km, then continue along this towpath for roughly 5km further (passing the Claverton Pumping Station on the way) heading towards the Dundas Aqueduct.

Cross the canal on Bridge 177 to Avoncliff. The path then immediately winds around a stone Waterways building, continuing left over the swing bridge where you parted from the canal earlier. Continue over the **Dundas Aqueduct** and along the right bank of the canal towpath to the **Avoncliff Aqueduct**, using the underpass to gain the towpath on the far side. Continue on this side of the canal back to **Bradford on Avon**.

Beware joining traffic from the right.

Beware the roundabout cunningly disguised as a central fountain.

ROUTE 7

Bourton-on-the-Water Loop via Great Barrington

Start/Finish	War memorial, village green, Bourton-on-the-Water (SP 168 207)
Distance	26km (16 miles)
Total ascent/descent	415m
Grade	Moderate
Terrain	70% roads, 30% off-road
Refreshments	The Lamb Inn (Great Rissington); The Fox Inn (Great Barrington); several in Bourton
Parking	Village car parks, Bourton (fee)
Cycle hire	Bourton or TY Cycles (mobile)
Road bikes?	Yes, but with significant detours on the outward stretch to avoid off-road sections (follow Route 22, Day 3 from Bourton, then continue along the road from Great Rissington to Great Barrington).
Connecting routes	Routes 4 and 18

A short and easy route taking you high onto a ridgeline south of Bourton, featuring some great off-road tracks and a fast descent back to the start.

To stay **on road**, turn right here (see map) to Little Rissington and through Great Rissington on country lanes, eventually rejoining the main route just north of Great Barrington.

Head S along High Street, passing a cycle hire shop on your left. At the end of this road turn left opposite Halford House. ◄ Continue past the petrol station/coach parking, and where the road bends left take the next right (Roman Way). Turn right onto Moor Lane, following Oxfordshire Way signs.

Where the track bends sharp left towards **Moors Farm**, turn right onto a smaller track then left through a wooden gateway (after roughly 200m), following Wyck Rissington signs.

This takes you through **Greystones Farm/ Salmondsbury Meadow Nature Reserve**. These are rare examples of wildflower meadows in the Cotswolds, most of which have not survived the introduction of modern farming practices using chemical fertilisers. Some here have survived due to being farmed traditionally; others are being restored to their former (summer) glory, although this takes centuries rather than years.

Continue through two fields, leaving the nature reserve just before crossing over a stream on a sleeper bridge. Cross the middle of a large hay meadow and

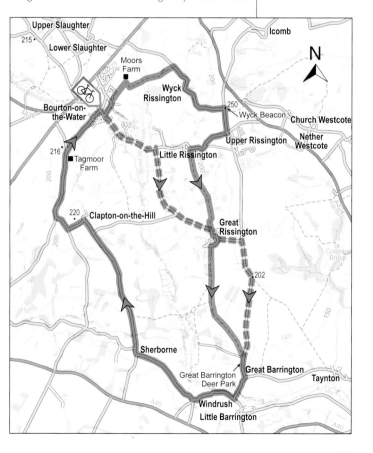

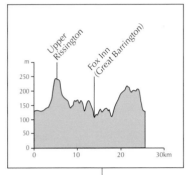

over another sleeper bridge. Bend left through two small hay meadows (the bridleway gets a bit rough here), then turn right up a country lane and into **Wyck Rissington**. This passes the church and bends a few times before heading steeply uphill to Wyck Beacon.

Turn right at the T-junction and then right at the first junction (of a double junction) on the edge of **Upper Rissington**, now descending into **Little Rissington**. ◀

Mountain bikers will note that the route has climbed a hill to avoid a bridleway. Sadly the bridleway gets very boggy and hoof-holed, and it has a rough and surprisingly steep uphill after the muddy ford across the stream.

Don't get too carried away with the descent: turn sharp left onto Pound Lane as the major road bends sharp right near the start of the village. Follow a track towards **Great Rissington**, descending for roughly 1.6km, gently at first and more steeply nearer the dip in the bottom. Partway down the gentle descent the track becomes somewhat rutted, but pick your line carefully and you can avoid the worst. On the steeper descent the surface becomes stonier but the best line is clearer.

Ignore two private roads near the bottom of the dip. Where the obvious stony track bends right at the second of these, continue ahead on a grassy field edge, bending

Bridleway between Little Rissington and Great Rissington

Fallow deer in Great Barrington Deer Park

right through a gap in the hedge at its end. Descend briefly then bend sharp left and go through a small gate onto a more distinct farm track. A proliferation of tracks occurs by the first farm building; head slightly right and gently downhill to exit through a driveway gate.

Turn left onto a village lane and immediately bend rightwards towards The Barringtons. Bend left and go steeply up a short hill into **Great Rissington**, passing The Lamb PH as the gradient eases. Immediately past this, turn right onto a minor road. Just as you begin to enjoy the descent take a slightly hidden side-turn left (dead-end lane) by Holly Cottage.

Ignore all side-tracks for roughly 1km (SP 198 162). Here the main track on the ground bears right; ignore this and continue straight ahead along a grassy field edge just left of a narrow strip of woodland. Go through a small wooden gate at the end of the field and descend to go across a junction of tracks onto a well-defined vehicle track. Follow this steeply down a dip and up the far side and continue to meet a road on a junction with a dead-end lane.

Turn right along the road and descend past the deer park into **Great Barrington**. Bend right by the war memorial, cross over both braids of the river and turn sharp right onto a minor road opposite The Fox Inn. Continue through **Windrush**, bending right by the church and left by the red phone box.

Now continue rising slightly to the village of **Sherborne**, staying on the major road until it bends sharp left. Turn right here (effectively going straight ahead) to Clapton. Cross the river then rise up a short but steep section of hill.

> **Sherborne Water Meadows** – a rare example of restored water meadows – are a short detour from here. A series of ditches and sluices allow river water to reach and improve a large area of meadow, which then provides rich grazing for sheep. Counter-intuitively, the water's main purpose is not irrigation but to warm the soil gently in early spring, hastening the start of the growing season. However, fertile silt carried in from the river was an added bonus. Being a labour-intensive method of farming, water meadows fell into decline with the advent of modern fertilisers.

After this the lane appears level, but it is still rising gently and will feel harder work than it looks.

As you enter **Clapton-on-the-Hill** turn left towards Bourton-on-the-Water. Gently descend to a T-junction and turn right, still heading towards Bourton. Continue along this ridgeline lane for nearly 2km.

Shortly after passing the driveway to **Tagmoor Farm**, the major road bends right (to Bourton – village only), but most traffic is encouraged to turn left. Stay right and enjoy a great descent on a narrow lane into **Bourton**, continuing along the major road (Sherborne Street) as you enter the village. Pass the Duke of Wellington PH and cross over a low river bridge to reach High Street.

ROUTE 8
Kemble via Cotswold Water Park

Start/Finish	The Tavern Inn, by Kemble railway station (ST 985 975)
Distance	32km (20 miles)
Total ascent/descent	120m
Grade	Moderate
Terrain	77% roads, 23% off-road
Refreshments	On route: The Greyhound PH (Siddington); Royal Oak PH (South Cerney) Short detour: various pubs in Ewen, South Cerney, Cricklade, Leigh, Somerford Keynes and Minety; café at Keynes Country Park Visitor Centre
Parking	On-road in Kemble village
Cycle hire	Somerford Keynes, Lechlade, Stroud, Stonehouse or mobile providers
Road bikes?	Water park tracks can get very muddy after prolonged wet weather (it was impassably flooded in summer 2012), and even in dry conditions can be quite bumpy. Road bikes are not suitable for this section – a possible detour could be via Cerney Wick to Ashton Keynes.
Connecting routes	Route 12
Note	Some of the country lanes marked on the map are actually very wide rat runs, and not particularly suited to cycling. This route does everything it can to avoid them, but many of the 'short detour' pubs and cafés will involve their use. A short detour at Neigh Bridge Country park is currently required to avoid a very overgrown bridleway section.

This route features plenty of quiet country lanes (mostly where heavy lorries are banned) to and from the Cotswold Water Park – a wildlife haven on former gravel quarries.

From the Tavern Inn, bend left across the railway bridge. Turn right (now joining NCN45) at a T-junction; this brings you to two staggered crossroads – the first over the A429 and the second over a quieter road that is often surprisingly awkward to cross due to limited visibility to the left. Cross both of these and continue ahead to Ewen, passing the exit of Washpool Lane early on.

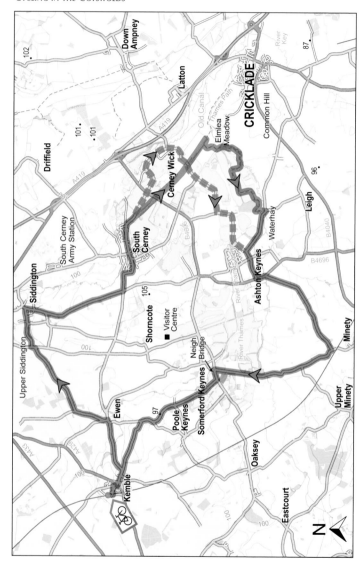

Take the first through road left in **Ewen** (towards Siddington, with a thatched cottage on the corner). Stay on this road for roughly 3km. Turn left towards Cirencester and then take the next right towards **Upper Siddington** (leaving NCN45). Continue in the village to the end of this road, opposite a convenience store. Turn right and continue for roughly 2.5km.

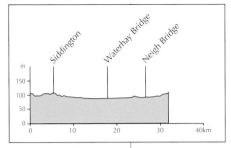

Turn left at the crossroads (ignore 'Welcome to Cotswold Water Park' signs ahead), and follow the major road as it twists and turns through the village of **South Cerney**. ▶

Towards the eastern end you get your first glimpse of the water parks by the gate to Lake 16 (private), just after a side-turn left to Wildmoorway Lane. Cross the road and take a bridleway just left of this gate, running parallel to the road and rejoining NCN45 (which crosses the road at this

This is an ancient village, known to have existed before the Domesday book, with a parish charter issued by King Aethelred II (the Unready) in AD999.

Bridleway at the start of the water parks near South Cerney

To stay **on road**, continue on this road to Cerney Wick (see map) and then follow signs to Ashton Keynes.

point). ◄ This narrow and sometimes muddy track continues over an access road to South Cerney Sailing Club; go between two lakes to emerge next to a car park by a redbrick bridge.

Continue under the bridge and cross the busy B4696. Continue on the Sustrans path for roughly 2.2km, passing under a further redbrick bridge, then turn right at a signposted junction onto the Thames Path (Sustrans-like bridleway). This runs past Elmlea Meadow.

> **Elmlea meadow** – a SSSI – has never suffered chemical fertilisation. Look out for the once-common yellow iris and brown hawker dragonfly among other local rarities (including pipistrelle bats).

The track bends right then left at a junction of tracks. Soon after this, turn right onto a narrower path (still continuing on the Thames Path) where a footpath continues ahead (on the wider track). The path now runs just right of a fenced-in grassy field, then crosses a bridge over a small stream. Bend left here and follow the path as it

The lakes here are imaginatively named – this is the view over 'Lake 72'

twists and turns around the lakes, crossing over a private road access after about 1km.

> In winter, or after prolonged wet conditions, this section from Elmlea to the private road access can get impassably **flooded**; even in the dry a few pot-holes (avoidable) are surprisingly deep and take a long time to dry out. In dry conditions it's worth a 300m detour right at the left-hand bend to the Cleveland Lakes bird hide (at SU 073 948).

Continue along the path, which continues to twist and turn, to a junction of bridleways. Turn left (initially staying on the Thames Path, but this soon turns right and becomes just a footpath), and go through Waterhay Bridge car park. Turn right onto the lane ahead.

Follow this into **Ashton Keynes** and bend left to reach a crossroads. Cross this (towards Minety) then turn left onto the B4696. Fork right on a left-hand bend after roughly 300m. Follow this lane for nearly 3km to a T-junction on the edge of Minety. Turn right towards **Somerford Keynes** and continue for roughly 3km to a very wide and busy road (Spine Road West).

Cross this road and turn left into Neigh Bridge Car Park. Follow the car park to reach an old bit of road and follow this briefly left to its end. Dismount to walk over the next 80m or so and remount to follow a minor road on the right (to Old Mill Farm).

Seasonal variant

Outside the nesting season, when the bridleway should be clear, the busy road and dismount can be avoided by taking a bridleway (roughly 300m before the junction) heading NW, then turning right to use a very short bit of the busy road to reach the Old Mill Farm road.

Turn right towards Ewen and take the next left to Kemble. This exits Washpool Lane 300–400m outside Kemble village. Turn left; retrace your outward route over a couple of crossroads and go left into Station Road.

ROUTE 9
Kingham Loop via Bruern Abbey

Start/Finish	Kingham railway station (SP 257 227)
Distance	28km (18 miles)
Total ascent/descent	255m
Grade	Moderate
Terrain	64% roads, 36% off-road
Refreshments	Choice of pubs in Kingham; The Chequers PH (Churchill); Café de la Post (Chadlington); Swan Inn (Ascott-under-Wychwood); Shaven Crown Hotel (Shipton-under-Wychwood)
Parking	Kingham railway station (fee)
Cycle hire	Bourton-on-the-Water or TY Cycles (mobile)
Road bikes?	Requires significant detours to avoid off-road sections
Connecting routes	Route 3
Note	There is a short section of fast A-road (less than 100m) on this route, and the right turn off it is awkward. While the route avoids the wettest of the woodland bridleways, it is perhaps best done in dry conditions.

This is a more serious off-road venture than the previous routes, exploring lovely bridleways alongside the River Evenlode and through Bruern Abbey. In Churchill look out for the memorial to the Father of Geology, and a surprisingly grand village church.

Turn left out of the railway station access road and continue over the railway bridge past Langston Priory Workshops. As the road bends right, turn left to the long village of **Kingham**. Look for Churchill's church dominating the skyline to your right as you enter the village.

The road twists and turns; immediately beyond the third PH (Kingham Plough), turn right then bend left around a green. Turn right at a T-junction, and just before the road bends sharp right turn left onto a dirt track bridleway (entrance not obvious until you're almost past it). Follow this to reach a junction (and tarmac again). ◄

To stay **on road** continue along this road into Churchill.

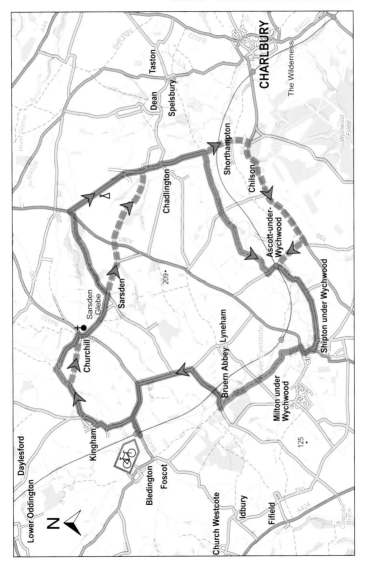

71

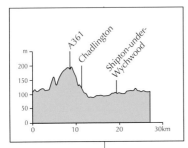

Turn right, climbing to **Churchill**. At the hilltop turn right at a T-junction by the memorial to William Smith.

William Smith (1769–1839) came to be known as the 'Father of British Geology'. Having trained as a surveyor, his major contribution to geological science was the discovery that rock strata could be identified as a unique layer by the fossils contained within it. From this he was able to identify where the same layer of rocks occurred

Memorial to William Smith in the village of Churchill

in different places. In 1815 he published the first map of the geology of England, Wales and (parts of) Scotland, which forms the basis of most modern-day geological maps of Britain.

Now continue along this road to the grand and imposing church.

It's worth a brief detour to see this surprisingly **grand building**. The church tower is apparently a smaller-scale replica of the tower of Magdalen College, and the rest of the church owes a lot of its design to that of various other Oxford colleges.

Immediately beyond the church turn left towards Sarsden. Enjoy the descent and continue towards Chipping Norton. Pass Sarsden Glebe Farm's driveway and turn left onto a dead-end lane at a minor cross-roads. ▸ As this ends by a private driveway, continue straight ahead past a wooden bollard onto a dirt track. Follow this across some woodland then on a track to the left of the continuation woodland to reach a busy main road (A361).

Turn left onto this, then right to **Chadlington** roughly 100m later. ▸ Continue into Chadlington and cross a staggered major crossroads towards Charlbury on Horseshoe Road, passing a café on the corner.

Shortly before the road bends sharp left to cross the river, turn right onto a bridleway (Oxfordshire Way). ▸ Follow this along the edge of fields for roughly 1.5km. You will cross a stream on a small concrete bridge early on; the way then dodges slightly right and then left before continuing ahead again.

Cross a country lane and follow the continuation bridleway along a vehicle track. As the track fades, bend fractionally left and follow a line of trees and wooden posts. Follow the edge of the next field as it bends right to pass a garage-like structure on your right. Continue straight ahead across the middle of a grassy meadow on a faint path, then beside the wall of the next meadow,

To stay **on road**, continue along this road, dog leg left then right over A361 then turn right to Chadlington.

Take care: this is a blind junction on a busy road.

To stay **on road**, continue along this road, then turn right along the B4437. After roughly 3km, turn right to Ascott-under-Wychwood.

The Oxfordshire Way bridleway runs through fields near Ascott-under-Wychwood

eventually crossing a tiny stream on a slabby bridge (SP 304 198).

Turn left and follow the edge of the next two fields, ignoring a bridge over the river on your left. As vehicle tracks become more prominent, veering uphill and rightwards, take a narrow track leftwards through field-edge vegetation to reach a road.

Turn left onto this and into **Ascott-under-Wychwood village**. Cross a railway (level crossing), turning right immediately after this onto Shipton Road. Continue out of the village with a bend left then right. At the edge of **Shipton** turn right (to effectively go straight ahead) at a T-junction on a bend. Reach a T-junction with the A361 and turn right towards Banbury.

After a sharp bend right (still in the village), turn left onto Meadow Lane, continuing ahead when it becomes a dirt bridleway. Where this fades to a grassy track and a footpath continues ahead, bend sharp left and go slightly uphill. As the gradient eases and a footpath joins from the left, turn right then bend left through the middle of a field. Continue across a couple of grassy fields and onto a track between fences to reach a road. ◀

This section of bridleway can be slow to dry.

Cross this and continue onto a track between fences (bridleway). Now follow the left edge of a field, go through a gap in trees at the far end of this, and continue straight ahead on a wide grassy strip between trees (ignoring other tracks crossing over). Cross a wildflower meadow, then a grassy field. Almost opposite Bruern Abbey House the bridleway bears diagonally left. ▸ Exit through a small wooden gate onto a country lane.

> Avoid a much more obvious track (footpath) continuing straight ahead along the fenceline.

> **Bruern Abbey** was founded as a Cistercian Abbey in 1147. Little remains of this now; the current manor house was built in classic Baroque style around 1720 for Sir John Cope, then MP for Banbury.

Do not take the continuation bridleway here – it rapidly bogs out and barely dries, even in prolonged dry weather. Instead turn right onto the lane and bend several times through Bruern hamlet, crossing over the river and railway (level crossing). Rise up gently to a T-junction and begin to follow signs to Kingham, here turning left onto a wide road. Follow this to a T-junction with the B4450 and turn left. Stay on the major road as it bends left at the turn to Kingham and continue to the station entrance.

ROUTE 10
Batheaston Sting

Start/Finish	Bottom of Penthouse Hill, just off High Street, Batheaston (ST 778 675)
Distance	14km (9 miles)
Total ascent/descent	440m
Grade	Moderate
Terrain	100% roads (but can be rough/muddy in places)
Refreshments	Short detour: The While Lion PH (Batheaston); several in Bathford/Bathhampton/northern Bath area
Parking	Very limited parking on road in Batheaston/Northend
Cycle hire	Bath, Bradford, Bristol or Chippenham (Lacock)
Road bikes?	Yes, but see note on Terrain
Connecting routes	Route 6
Note	This route is all about the ascents, not the descents, as the roads are extremely narrow and twisty and it's hard to pick up much speed safely on steep descents. The route follows 200m of main road to cross the A46.

A short hill challenge route, ideal for a quick ride out with maximum effort and minimal time. It is described in the easiest direction for those new to hills; for a tougher workout reverse the route or take the left fork rather than the right at Hollies Lane.

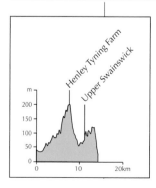

Head up Penthouse Hill; this quiet lane is initially steep but the gradient soon eases before a somewhat unexpected descent, levelling out through a traffic-calmed residential area.

This marks the start of a **generally undulating section** of the route, where the uphills are steep but short-lived, followed by an enjoyable descent that feels like it's losing far more height than it really is, as you ascend gently overall rather than relentlessly.

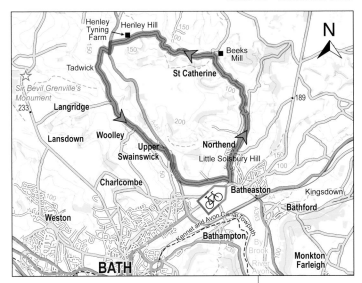

Now I could simply say 'continue on the major road for 7.4km'! Instead, continue straight ahead at Hollies Lane. ▶ Continue past the exit of Ramscombe Lane (where the variant rejoins); the next significantly steep (but short) hill starts soon after this.

> Whichever fork you take you will notice the very grand and imposing building of **St Catherine's Court** on your left. It is of 15th-century origin and Grade II listed, although the manor has been extended and remodelled over the centuries. Rumour alleges that King Henry VIII's illegitimate daughter was raised here. More recently owned by actress Jane Seymour, it has been rented out as a film set and recording studio to bands such as Radiohead and Robbie Williams, before becoming a private mansion for hire by the day.

Shortly after the church the road bends sharp left and descends briefly. ▶ The next section is surprisingly

To make the route harder, take Hollies Lane to add further ascent and descent, turning right onto Ramscombe Lane at the 'dead-end' crossroads.

On the next uphill the left bank can be somewhat prone to small landslides.

77

The lanes around the hamlet of St Catherine are very narrow and quiet

undulating, with short steep ascents and unexpected descents.

On a twisty section, shortly after the driveway to Beeks Mill on the right, the lane does a sharp bend left and rises steeply. This is the start of the main ascent, although the gradient does relent in a few places, with a good view across the valley rightwards at the first easing of the gradient. Ignore a tarmac farm track leading to the right as you pass a widening in the road by a farm (**Henley Tyning**). Shortly after this, gravity briefly aids a final short push to the summit.

At the top turn left onto a main road (A46). Fortunately this section is short – after roughly 200m turn right to Tadwick. ◀ A gentle descent soon steepens after a sharp bend left. Take the left fork where the road splits and continue the very steep and narrow descent into **Tadwick**. The gradient briefly eases towards the end of the village, and as a second descent eases out the way becomes generally undulating. Ignore three side-turns to the right and rise to a joining of lanes at a small triangular green in **Upper Swainswick**. Ignore the left turns and continue on the main lane.

A layby eases the way on this section for those not used to riding on main roads.

At a T-junction near the A46 sliproad, turn right and enjoy a short descent to a minor road on the left that takes you under the A46. Turn right immediately after this, heading parallel with the A46 before bending left and heading gently uphill, with a good view over Bath. A narrow, steep descent to a T-junction follows; turn right and rejoin the outgoing route, with a final short and steep descent.

The final ascent to the A46 from Henley Tyning Farm

ROUTE 11
Stratford Greenway Loop via Mickleton

Start/Finish	Seven Meadows (Greenway) car park, Stratford-upon-Avon (SP 196 540)
Distance	42km (26 miles)
Total ascent/descent	320m
Grade	Moderate
Terrain	61% roads, 35% trails, 4% off-road
Refreshments	On route: Masons Arms (Pebworth); Butchers Arms (Mickleton); Red Lion and Howard Arms (Ilmington) Short detour: several in Stratford; Carriages Café (Stratford end of The Greenway); Masons Arms (Long Marston, 200m); Barn Tea Rooms and College Arms (Lower Quinton)
Parking	Car park at start point (free)
Cycle hire	Stratford
Road bikes?	Mostly OK for sturdy bikes with care; bridleway over Nebsworth easily avoided if necessary.
Connecting routes	Route 2
Note	To access the trail from the railway station, head right then pick up NCN5 to reach the Greenway.

A gentle warm-up on the Stratford Greenway is followed by a stiff hill with fantastic views over the surrounding countryside. Stiff hills, of course, usually mean great descents – and the one into Ilmington is no exception.

Leave the far end of the car park on the Greenway cycle track, passing a couple of old carriages now used as a cycle hire centre and café. This long cycle track crosses over several gravel tracks/roads along its length, not mentioned directly here. In the first 4km it runs past the racecourse and across the rivers Avon (large bridge) and Stour (small bridge) before reaching a road crossing. Cross this and continue for a further 3km to Wyre Crossing.

Turn right along a gravel track (Wyre Lane) by a cream-coloured house. This soon gains tarmac and leads to **Long Marston**.

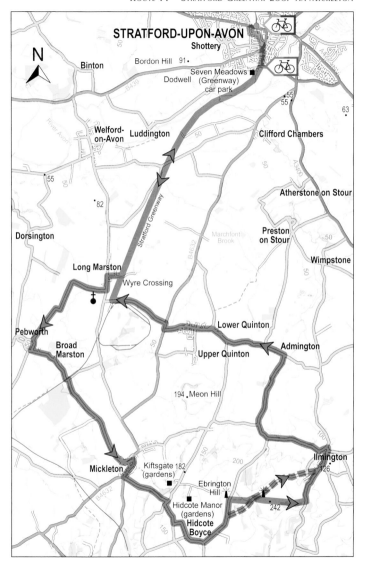

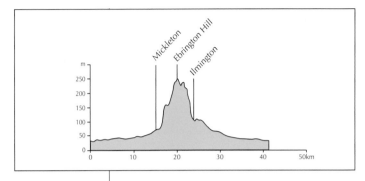

Riding across the former rail bridge over the River Avon on the edge of Stratford

The Greenway is a former railway line – the northern end of the **Honeybourne line** to Stratford. It was originally built by the Oxford Worcester and Wolverhampton Railway, a company whose reputation was so bad they were nicknamed Old Worse and Worse. Eventually taken over by the GWR, the line was finally closed in 1976.

Turn left at the T-junction, and towards the end of the village turn right to **Pebworth**, opposite a red postbox.

Continue past the church and take the next left. As you enter Pebworth turn left onto Friday Street, towards Broad Marston.

Local legend has it that one night **William Shakespeare** joined a group of Stratford folks aiming to outdo a drinking club from nearby Bidford. They lost the contest, and when a re-match was suggested for the following night Shakespeare declined, saying he had drunk at 'piping Pebworth, dancing Marston, haunted Hillbro, hungry Grafton, dudging Exhall, papist Wixford, beggarly Broom and drunken Bidford', and would not continue. Whether or not this is true remains unclear, but Pebworth is still known as a Shakespeare village.

Turn left to **Mickleton**, entering Broad Marston very soon afterwards. Continue out of the village beside fields, go under a railway bridge and bend sharp left. Roughly 50m beyond this bend (not the gravel track next to the bridge), turn right to Mickleton.

Reaching Mickleton, bend left by a former spring and continue past the Butchers Arms PH to a T-junction opposite the village stores. Turn right towards Cheltenham (B4632) and continue to a mini-roundabout on the edge of the village. Cross straight over this and immediately turn left towards Hidcote and Kiftsgate. The hill climb now begins, gently at first but soon in earnest.

At a T-junction turn right towards **Hidcote Boyce** (or detour left to view the Hidcote or Kiftsgate gardens). Bend left where a road marked 'unsuitable for motors' turns right. Enjoy a brief downhill, passing the once-grand Hidcote House (not to be confused with the National Trust-owned Hidcote Manor Gardens less than 1km away).

Take the next road left towards Ilmington. Bend sharp right at the top (do not go straight ahead on the farm access track); this marks the start of the second steep

On a clear day you can see Broadway Tower on the distant skyline from here.

To stay **on road**, stay on thie road (see map) all the way to Ilmington.

Sturdy road bikes will be able to pick their way through this descent with care, but may find both this and the previous muddy section challenging.

ascent of the day. As the gradient steepens by a minor road, continue straight ahead towards Ilmington on a sustained ascent. ◄

At a T-junction at the top, turn left towards Ilmington and rise very gently for a further 1km. The road bends left as the gradient eases significantly. Very shortly after this, as the major road bends right, turn left onto a minor road (unsigned). ◄ Continue to the true top of the hill (almost level at this point) by some radio transmitters. This is Ebrington Hill – the highest point in Warwickshire at 259m.

Turn right opposite these onto a pleasant singletrack bridleway to a small gate at the far end of a grassy field. Cross the road beyond and continue ahead on a stony track leading briefly uphill. The gradient eases again by the masts, the track now running between hedges surrounded by fields. Enjoy a steep descent to a gate where a footpath crosses the track. Continue ahead – the surface briefly becomes more level, and sometimes muddy – then descend steeply on a somewhat rough stony surface to reach a road. ◄ Turn left onto this and enjoy a fantastic descent into **Ilmington**.

Turn right at the oblique junction at the bottom of the road and descend past the Red Lion and Howard Arms pubs. Continue on the major road around a sharp bend left.

Take the next left towards **Admington**. Soon after Larkstoke Cottage the lane becomes twistier. At a sharp bend left, turn right to Admington on a narrower lane and then turn left to Quinton at a T-junction at the end of the village. Gently ascend, rejoining NCN5 as you enter **Lower Quinton**.

Bend left past the College Arms and go through a traffic-calmed area near the primary school. At a T-junction with the B4632 use a cycle track to turn right (avoiding, then crossing, the B-road towards Long Marston). After roughly 1.6km turn right onto the Greenway (at its southernmost end) and continue back to your start point.

ROUTE 12

Cirencester Loop via Ampney Crucis

Start/Finish	Outside St John's Church, Cirencester (SP 023 020)
Distance	33km (21 miles)
Total ascent/descent	300m
Grade	Moderate
Terrain	94% roads, 6% off-road
Refreshments	On route: plenty in Cirencester; Hare & Hounds PH (Foss Cross); Crown of Crucis (Ampney Crucis) Short detour: The Greyhound (Siddington)
Parking	On Sheep Street, or at The Waterloo car park (fee)
Cycle hire	Somerford Keynes, Lechlade, Stroud, Stonehouse, Cheltenham or mobile providers
Road bikes?	Yes, with a detour from Akeman Street to Siddington.
Connecting routes	Routes 8, 13, 14 and 18
Note	The one-way system in Cirencester will confound most attempts on a bicycle to avoid the busy roads. The route described here is perhaps the only way across from south to north without having to either dismount or encounter the chaotic oval roundabout on the west of town.

This route uses the historic town of Cirencester as a start point and offers a good mix of quiet lanes and off-road bridleways once out of town. Some of the roadside verges have a delightful display of wildflowers in summer.

Head W along the marketplace, getting into the right-hand lane by the traffic lights. Turn right onto West Market Street (you are now following NCN48 signs all the way to Coln Rogers). Pass a narrowing and continue until the road makes a sharp bend right and becomes Spitalgate Lane.

Spitalgate Lane is so called due to the presence of St John the Evangelist **hospital and cloisters** – founded and endowed by Henry I in AD1133. You can see its remnants on the left near the start of the lane.

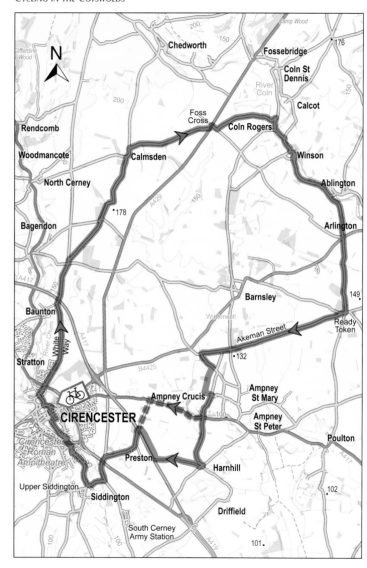

Continue straight ahead over a crossroads with traffic lights onto the 'White Way'. The road continues for just over 2km and then bends right to cross a dual carriageway on a flyover.

Continue over a minor crossroads and head right onto a lovely little country lane. ▶ Continue along this for roughly 3km, crossing over a minor road to reach

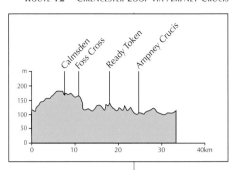

In summer this has lots of lovely flowers along it, particularly at the start.

The front section of St John's Church has been dominant on the marketplace since the cleaning of its golden sandstone blocks

87

Calmsden after a short descent. Turn right to enter the village proper, rise up gently through the village and bend right towards Fossebridge.

At Foss Cross, turn left onto a major road (A429) and then turn right opposite the Hare and Hounds PH before taking the next left to **Coln Rogers**. Enjoy the descent into the village, then turn right to Winson.

Stay on the main road to cross the river and enter the long village of **Winson**. ◄ Cross back over the river and turn left to 'Winson village only'. Continue past the triangular-shaped village green and rise gently to a T-junction. Turn left towards Bibury. At a junction on the edge of **Ablington** continue straight across towards Barnsley.

At a five-way junction take a minor road towards Poulton. At a crossroads at the tiny hamlet of **Ready Token**, turn right (initially towards Barnsley) and stay on the major road for roughly 4km. ◄

> There is some dispute as to the origins of **Ready Token**'s unusual name. Local author J Arthur Gibbs (1867–1899) suggested that it may be a corruption of Anglo-Saxon and Celtic words meaning 'on the way to the ford' (the River Colne ford at Fairford); more commonly it is thought to be derived from a pub in this hamlet that would not give credit – 'Ready Token' here meaning 'requiring cash payment'.

After a long section with no side-roads you encounter three fairly close together. ◄ Take the third left, at the bottom of a moderately steep descent, towards **Ampney Crucis**. ◄ Climb a short, steep, but shady hill, and just before a left turn take a stony track right between two large hedges.

Join a tarmac track on a bend by a large corrugated iron building. Turn left and then turn right and right again by a small triangular green. Continue ahead towards Driffield at a junction with the A417 by the Crown of Crucis PH. At the next T-junction turn right towards Preston, then almost immediately go right again onto a

Herons can often be seen waiting patiently for fish on this river.

This is Akeman Street – a former Roman road linking the Fosse Way to Watling Street near St Albans.

To stay **on road**, continue to meet the B4425, head W along this and then S from a crossroads with the A429, doglegging right then left across the A417.

Don't confuse an earlier left turn to 'the Ampneys' with this one, and it's best to keep the speed down a bit in the dip to avoid missing the turning!

The view back towards Ampney from the bridleway joining the cut-off road to Preston

dead-end country lane. (Confusingly there are two A417 roads here: the main road you've just encountered and the dual carriageway ring road you'll encounter next.)

The ring road cuts the road off here, so turn right onto a narrow bridleway. This joins a tarmac track after roughly 500m; stay on this until it bends left to join a country lane. Turn left and cross a bridge over the ring road. Continue through **Preston** and as you exit the village turn left at the T-junction towards Cirencester. Cross over the main road almost immediately ahead. ▶ Shortly after a house called The Dairy Barn, turn right to Siddington and cross a small river.

This is more straightforward than it first appears.

In **Siddington** turn right onto Ashton Road. Follow this to the edge of town; when through traffic is signposted left around a bend, go straight ahead onto the dead-end continuation of Siddington Road.

Take the next left onto Kingsmead and use a narrow underpass to cross the dual carriageway. Rejoin the road opposite Kwik-Fit and turn right. Stay on the major road as it bends left, continuing past a couple of schools.

Roughly 300m after the second school (Paternoster), and shortly before some traffic lights (just in view), turn right onto The Avenue. Take the next left onto Tower Street and go over a major crossroads onto South Way, now following brown signs towards the Corinium Museum. This twists and turns; just beyond The Bear Inn turn left at a T-junction onto Dyer Street and head back to Market Place and your start point.

ROUTE 13
Filkins Loop via Bibury

Start/Finish	Woollen mill, Filkins (SP 239 044)
Distance	37km (23 miles)
Total ascent/descent	310m
Grade	Moderate
Terrain	67% roads, 33% off-road
Refreshments	On route: woollen mill café (Filkins); village shop café (Coln St Aldwyns), Victoria Inn (Eastleach Turville) Short detour: The Sherbourne Arms PH (Aldsworth), William Morris tea room and The Catherine Wheel PH (Bibury); New Inn PH (Coln St Aldwyns); The Keepers Arms (Quenington); Five Alls PH (Filkins)
Parking	On road in Filkins (limited space)
Cycle hire	Woollen Weavers in Filkins (see Lechlade in Appendix B); Bourton, Somerford Keynes or mobile
Road bikes?	Requires a significant detour from the start to Aldsworth (using B4425), and a similar detour north of Bibury.
Connecting routes	Routes 12, 14 and 18
Note	Detours to avoid off-road sections may well involve use of main roads (for example B4425).

Starting in a quiet, off-the-beaten track village, the route then stays off-road as much as it reasonably can while visiting some pretty villages. Bibury in particular is one of the deserved honeypots of the Cotswolds.

To stay **on road** for the first half of today's route, set off south east from Filkins towards Broadwell, turn left to Kencot and follow the dashed route line on the map as far as Aldsworth.

◄ Head N from the woollen centre for just over 800m, then take a bridleway (d'Arcy Dalton Way) left towards Holwell.

The **d'Arcy Dalton Way** is a relatively new long-distance footpath. It is 66 miles long and meanders from Wormleighton in Warwickshire to Wayland's Smithy in Oxfordshire. Colonel WP d'Arcy Dalton (after whom the route is named) was a key figure in preserving rights of way in Oxfordshire.

Cross over a main road (A361), continuing on the bridleway ahead. This begins as a stony track across a field and carries on in a fairly straight line for roughly 2.5km – either following field boundaries or striking across fields. Later, near Furze Ground, it becomes more enclosed

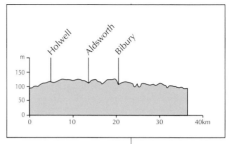

between walls or trees and reaches a country lane. ▶

Cross this country lane and continue on the bridleway across a field. Another bridleway joins from the left by a gate, but keep straight ahead along a track to reach a country lane on the edge of **Holwell**. Turn left along this, pass a house, and turn left down a 'restricted byway' track. This becomes tarmac after passing through the farmyard of Holwell Downs Farm, then continues to meet a country lane.

Turn left along this, go across a major crossroads (towards Eastleach Turville) and then turn right to

> Beware: it's easy to veer slightly too far left at the start of one of the middle fields where a left fork seems tempting, but the line continues straight ahead.

The Filkins to Holwell bridleway becomes increasingly enclosed between walls and trees near Furze Ground

91

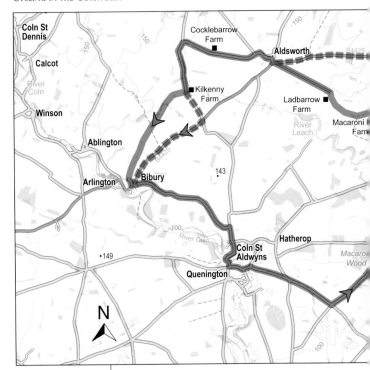

Eastleach Farm (only). The tarmac ends by the farm; the continuation bridleway is initially slightly rough and stony before becoming a lovely grassy track.

The farm below has the unusual name of **Macaroni Downs**. 'Downs' refers to the grassy rolling terrain, but the Macaroni bit is less obvious. Two versions of its origins involve racehorses on the long-abandoned Bibury racecourse between Eastleach and Ladbarrow farms: one suggests it was a group of Italians, the other that it was British royalty, whose racehorses were stabled and raced here. Either way,

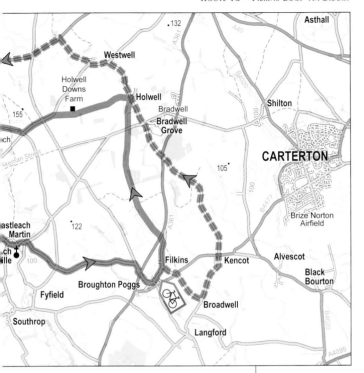

'Macaroni' relates to the racegoers sporting the latest high fashions of the 18th century.

It's easy to miss the left fork (SP 185 087) leading into the foot of a gentle hollow and through a large wooden gate. Continue past a waymarker and up a rise, bending right again now on a grassy strip across the middle of an arable field. Turn right onto a tarmac track, which brings you past the pretty front of Ladbarrow Farm house. Turn sharp left immediately after this house down a leafy dirt lane (soon becoming tarmac) to the edge of **Aldsworth**.

The Lavender Gardens of the Bibury Trout Farm (by the bridge) contribute significantly to its claim as 'the prettiest village in the Cotswolds'

Take a dog-leg left then right at a major crossroads in Aldsworth. Just past the war memorial turn left towards Eastington. Pass the entrance to Wall Farm at the edge of the village then turn left onto a surprisingly straight road towards Cocklebarrow. This continues for roughly 2km, descending then bending left before rising to a T-junction. Turn left and continue for roughly 1.2km.

To stay **on road**, stay on the road, turning right after about a kilometre for Bibury.

At the crest of a short rise, turn right onto a bridleway (track). ◄ Keep following this straight ahead, crossing a farm track then a single grassy field. ◄ Go through a small gate in front of a barn conversion, following an obvious line by a metal fence to emerge onto a tarmac lane. Continue down this, turning right onto the continuation bridleway at the end.

The line becomes very indistinct here.

As this track reaches a public road in **Bibury**, turn left then fork right to Coln St Aldwyns. ◄ Continue for roughly 3km then turn right. Cross over a more major road by the community café as you enter **Coln St Aldwyns**, descending past The New Inn PH to cross first a millrace, then the small River Coln. Rise up the steep (but short) hill into **Quenington**, turning left by a cemetery onto Fowlers

It's worth a detour, to the right along the main road, to see this pretty village and the trout farm by the north end of the river.

Lane. This then descends past a junction with Victoria Road near some wetland. Continue on the main road leftwards and across the River Coln once more.

Bridge over the River Coln in Bibury

Rise up the valley on the far side. At an oblique crossroads continue straight ahead towards Southrop. At the next junction turn left towards Macaroni Wood, then take the next right to **Eastleach Turville**. Continue through the village, descending to cross the small river by a church.

Almost immediately after this there is a confusing junction; turn right to take the minor road going straight up the hill towards Filkins. Continue over a minor crossroads then turn right towards Burford. Fork right to Filkins – this dips under the A361 – then turn left onto a major road and go back through the village.

ROUTE 14
Fairford Loop via Bibury

Start/Finish	St Mary's Church, Fairford (SP 152 012)
Distance	39km (24 miles)
Total ascent/descent	335m
Grade	Moderate
Terrain	69% roads, 31% off-road
Refreshments	On route: Catherine Wheel PH (Bibury); village shop café (Coln St Aldwyns) Short detour: several pubs and 7a Coffee Shop in Fairford; Red Lion PH (Ampney St Peter); William Morris tea room (Bibury); New Inn PH (Coln St Aldwyns); The Keepers Arms (Quenington)
Parking	Car park opposite St Mary's Church on Mill Lane (free)
Cycle hire	Lechlade, Bourton-on-the-Water, Somerford Keynes or mobile
Road bikes?	Yes, with a lot of detours. Suggested deviations include a short road section northwest from Fairford, and Winson/Calcot/Eastington from Ablington to Kilkenny Farm.
Connecting routes	Routes 12, 13 and 18

This the central route of a trio based around Bibury. It features plenty of easy to moderately challenging bridleways. Road riders can follow a broadly similar route with a large detour from Ablington.

An old steam engine is often visible here.

Head W along Mill Street towards Mill and Oxpens and cross the River Coln. At a T-junction turn right and continue for roughly 2km, eventually passing an old rusty windpump atop a water tower on your left. Turn left immediately beyond this onto a stony track (unsigned bridleway), which becomes a more maintained gravel track shortly before a large barn. ◄

At the end of this track turn right onto a country lane by Honeycomb Leaze Farm. After roughly 1km you'll reach an awkward five-way junction; take the major road left to Betty's Grave, then continue ahead at the Betty's Grave crossroads.

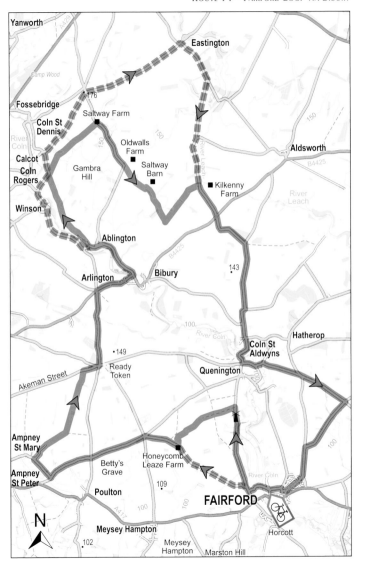

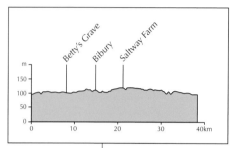

In the Middle Ages until roughly the mid-19th century, various groups of people were deemed unsuitable to be buried in a graveyard, and **crossroads** were often the alternative. This was particularly the case where the deceased were thought to be at greater risk of becoming ghosts, such as criminals who had been hanged, witches, and people who had committed suicide (which was considered to be both criminal and a sin). It is unclear who this particular Betty was; some sources suggest she was a local witch and others that she committed suicide after becoming pregnant out of wedlock.

Turn right at a minor crossroads to **Ampney St Mary**. In the village take the first right opposite a stone barn (just beyond a house called 'Indaba') and fork right at a small grassy triangle. Continue straight ahead where a tarmac track turns left, bending left then right a couple of times before tarmac cedes to stony track. This roughens slightly in a shallow dip. Continue straight ahead after this, eventually reaching Akeman Street nearly 3km from Ampney St Mary.

Turn right onto Akeman Street, then left at the minor crossroads in the hamlet of Ready Token. Head northwards for roughly 2km to reach another five-way junction. Turn right onto the B4425 to **Bibury** and descend into the village past the Catherine Wheel PH. Cross the river by the picturesque Bibury Trout Farm and turn left by the Swan Hotel to **Ablington**.

In the village, fork left towards Winson and then stay on the major road as it descends towards the River Coln. Don't cross the river, but shortly before this follow a tarmac track rightwards (with a sign for kennels). This soon becomes a stony track, which you follow for roughly 4km

in total, briefly meeting a road partway along. Early on there is a short awkward section where the track dips down to a stream (crossed on stepping stones as it is almost always slightly flooded) and then it climbs – first extremely steeply and then gently – on a rapidly improving stony surface to reach a bend in a country lane after roughly 2km. ▸

Emerge rightwards onto this and turn right immediately onto a further restricted byway with a rocky surface. Soon after another bridleway joins from the left the lane becomes a very pleasant grassy green lane, until a final short descent over rocky terrain to Saltway Farm.

Turn right along the lane, heading downhill. After roughly 1.6km, where the road bends sharp right, continue straight ahead on a vehicle track (restricted byway). ▸ The track becomes briefly vague near a small isolated brick building; bend left then right before this and go through a metal gateway to find the continuation track heading roughly SE. Follow this firm-based track to reach another junction of tracks. Turn sharp left here, almost back on yourself, and follow this good track to Kilkenny Farm.

Descending towards the road by Saltway Barn near Ablington

This stretch is very awkward for those unused to off-road riding, but doesn't last long.

This is one of many former 'salt ways', used to transport salt from Droitwich to the south of England.

The bridleway southeast of Oldwalls Farm runs over part of a former salt way

Turn right and follow this road to a crossroads with the B4425. Cross this, heading towards Coln St Aldwyns. At a T-junction turn right to **Coln St Aldwyns** and descend gently into the village.

Go over a major crossroads by the community shop/café and descend fairly steeply past The New Inn PH. Cross a millrace, then the small River Coln (again). Rise up the steep but short hill into **Quenington**, turning left by a cemetery onto Fowlers Lane. This then descends past a junction with Victoria Road near some wetland (which often floods). Bend leftwards on the major road and across the River Coln once more.

Rise up the valley on the far side, eventually continuing over a slightly staggered minor crossroads towards Southrop. At the next junction turn right to Fairford. Turn left at the T-junction, then fork right onto Hatherop Road at a triangular junction at the edge of Fairford. Continue along this road to its end and turn right at a T junction opposite a recreation ground. Take the next left (towards Poulton) to return to the start point.

ROUTE 15
Frampton Cotterell Loop via Wickwar

Start/Finish	Opposite The Globe PH, Frampton Cotterell (ST 667 820)
Distance	44km (28 miles)
Total ascent/descent	455m
Grade	Moderate
Terrain	91% roads, 9% off-road
Refreshments	On route: The Globe PH (Frampton Cotterell); Swan Inn PH (Tytherington); Severn View Farm (cakes and drinks – Inglestone Common); White Hart PH (Iron Acton). Also a café/bakery near the end (Frampton Cotterell) but beware very early closing times! Short detour: Swan Inn PH (Nibley); several in Wickwar
Parking	On road in one of several side streets in Frampton Cotterell (or in Flaxpits Lane free car park, Winterbourne)
Cycle hire	Bristol, Bradford, Stroud, Slimbridge or Lacock
Road bikes?	Yes – but see note
Connecting routes	No routes directly join, but Route 21 isn't far away
Note	The tracks above Hawkesbury and west of Horton were resurfaced in 2013. Currently most road bikes could manage the Hawkesbury track, and wider-tyred bikes the second, but they will degrade over time and were formerly poorly surfaced... The earlier bridleway (near Frampton Cotterell) was fine for road bikes at the time of writing. Access from Yate railway station is possible, but uses some busier/urban roads that aren't in character with the route. See map extract for line of detour.

The climb up to the Somerset Monument is steep, but the views you get from the track above Hawkesbury are ample reward.

Head W (away from the river bridge) up Church Road to a traffic light-controlled crossroads by a petrol station. Cross the B4058 here into Perrinpit Road, heading towards Almondsbury. Reach a sharp bend left after roughly 2km, just before a close-together pair of pylon lines.

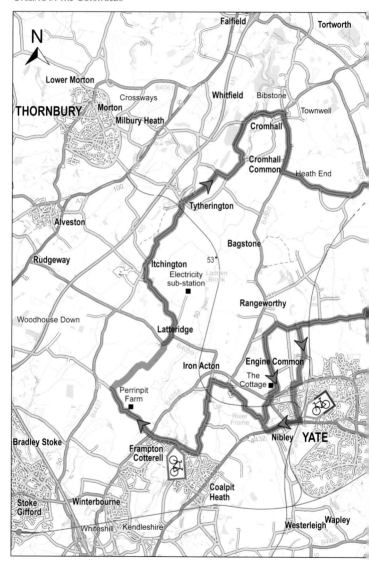

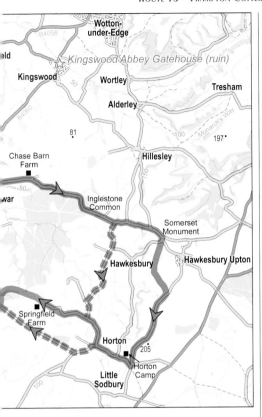

Turn right onto a bridleway just beyond this bend (**not** the footpath on the bend itself). This wide vehicle track bends sharp right and then left early on, with the track narrowing briefly between these bends. Bend right by a farmyard entrance then turn left at a T-junction of tracks and onto degraded tarmac. Follow this lane to a village green by a T-junction with the B4059.

Turn right, passing a duck pond after roughly 300m. Turn left immediately after this to Game Farm. After roughly 2km, as the road rises gently, turn right onto a

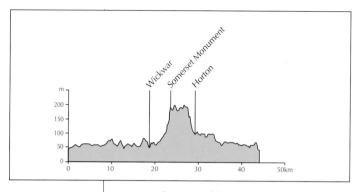

narrow weight-restricted lane just outside the tiny hamlet of **Itchington**.

Turn right at the T-junction and follow a winding lane for roughly 2km to **Tytherington**, going under the railway bridge and past The Swan PH. Take a dog-leg right then left over a major road into Baden Hill Road.

Turn right at the T-junction at the end. This is the first of the many times you will meet the Avon Cycleway (ACW) on this route; it is variously marked with brown cycle signs, NCN410 and 'Avon Cycleway'. (Here you will be following it for roughly 10km to Inglestone Common.)

Turn left at the next T-junction. After roughly 500m turn left onto a very minor road (easily missed). This continues for roughly 2.5km. Cross a stream and rise up past a minor road to the right.

Turn right onto the B4058 near **Cromhall**.

Cromhall has a disputed claim to fame as the place where one of the oldest **dinosaur fossils** was found – in the former Slickstones Quarry, 1.5km northeast of this junction. The fossils have been attributed to a specially-created genus (Agnosphitys cromhallensis) which has no other members, hence the controversy.

Continue along this for roughly 1.5km. Turn left onto Cowship Lane by a red telephone box. Continue ahead on this road for 2.8km. At a junction with a major road (B4059) turn right to **Wickwar**. Bend left, and at the edge of Wickwar rise up gently to a T-junction. Turn left (on the B4060) towards 'Old Cider Mill Trading Estate'.

High grassy plateaus used as common grazing, like Inglestone Common, are typical of the area around Stroud

As the road descends, fork second right (the one o'clock-ish turn) to Inglestone Common. Fork right by Chase Barn Farm after roughly 1.5km to stay on the through road. Continue for about 3km, crossing cattle grids at either end of the common, passing the driveway to Severn View Farm and leaving the ACW near the end of the common.

The road now steepens over the next 1km or so, passing a minor road to Hillesley and reaching a gradient of 1:7 at its steepest point. Continue up this lane to reach a monument at the top.

This is the **Somerset Monument**, erected four years after his death in memory of Lord Edward Somerset who was in charge of the Household Cavalry Brigade at Waterloo. It's now a Grade II* listed building.

The Somerset Monument, near Inglestone Common

Turn right past the memorial and descend gently into a hamlet. Turn first right (immediately before a bus stop on the right), then at the end of a triangle formed by the silted-up pond turn left onto a dirt track bridleway (Cotswold Way).

Continue along this lovely track, with great views over the valley below to the right, reaching a country lane after roughly 1.5km. Turn right onto this and descend gently past Horton Camp (an Iron Age hillfort) to a T-junction. Turn right, then bend sharp right and descend steeply into **Horton**.

As the gradient eases, turn right opposite Horton Social Club, rejoining the ACW very briefly once more. Where the through road forks right go straight ahead along Vinney Lane. The tarmac ends just after **Springfield Farm**; continue straight ahead on a restricted byway to reach a junction of tracks. Now on a bridleway, continue straight ahead, descending gently through woodland on a wide gravel track.

Rejoin tarmac on the public section of the driveway to Ladyswood House. Follow this rightwards to its end, turning right onto a country lane (Mapleridge Lane) and rejoining the ACW. Continue along here to reach a crossroads with the B4060.

Cross straight over this onto Bury Hill Lane towards Rangeworthy. Stay on this road for nearly 3km, crossing over a railway bridge, then turn right (still heading towards Rangeworthy) at a T-junction. As the road bends sharp right, turn left onto Chaingate Lane. Take the next left onto Dyers Lane and continue for roughly 1.5km. The road bends sharp right and then passes 'The Cottage'. Just after this house and just before some overhead power lines, turn left (very easily missed – if you reach a main road you've gone too far) onto a narrow minor lane. This ends after roughly 150m, just right of a roundabout on the edge of **Yate**.

> Yate was once the centre of UK mining for **celestium** – a variety of strontium that was mined for its use in refining sugar beet in the late 1800s and early 1900s, before it was discovered that when mixed with other chemicals it burned with a red flame, making it very useful as an additive to fireworks and flares. Industrial extraction ceased in the 1990s when the main workings were depleted, but small lumps of this pretty crystalline mineral can sometimes be seen gracing the gardens of Yate and its surrounding villages.

Cross over the more major road and onto a continuation cycle path opposite. After roughly 100m dog-leg right then left onto Bridge Road. Continue over the railway bridge, bending sharp right past a track incoming from the left (marked as a road on some maps). Turn right (opposite Hillcrest House) at the T-junction and go back over the railway.

On the edge of **Iron Acton village** turn left at a T-junction on a bend and continue through the village to a T-junction opposite The White Hart Inn. Turn left, then at a small triangular green, fork left on a minor road, soon passing over a level crossing. Continue along this lane to **Frampton Cotterell** (roughly 2km). Turn right at the T-junction and descend this wide and sometimes busy road to return to the start.

ROUTE 16

Stonehouse Loop via Slimbridge

Start/Finish	Junction of High Street and Regent Street, Stonehouse (SO 806 052)
Distance	43km (27 miles)
Total ascent/descent	450m
Grade	Moderate
Terrain	76% roads, 24% trails (including canalside and roadside paths)
Refreshments	On route: Woodchester snacks van (except Sundays and after 2.00pm); Rose and Crown Inn (Nympsfield); The George Inn (Frocester); Tudor Arms PH and The Black Shed café (Slimbridge); The Bell Inn (Frampton); Old Forge Inn (Whitminster) Short detour: several in Stonehouse, Stroud and Nailsworth (try Scrumptious café in Nailsworth or The Old Fleece PH on the A46 south of Stroud); Whitminster Inn (Whitminster, A38)
Parking	Station car park (fee), or on street behind the station
Cycle hire	Slimbridge, Stroud, Cheltenham, Painswick (electric bikes only) and choice of mobile services
Road bikes?	Sturdy road bikes capable of trail riding will be fine (although the trails can get muddy in wet conditions).
Connecting routes	Routes 19 and 22
Note	This route involves a short section of the A419 near Cam and Dursley station, and several main road crossings – some toucan-controlled, some not. The Gloucester and Sharpness Canal towpath is owned by the Canal and River Trust, who allow cycling at the time of writing.

The route starts very gently, later rising steeply across a broad hill near Nympsfield. A good descent follows; the canalside path is straightforward and the way is easy back to Stonehouse from there.

Descend Regent Street to the A419. Ignore a rare traffic light-controlled cycle crossing, instead using a toucan crossing to the left to cross the A419, following NCN45 signs towards Stroud.

You will be following NCN45 all the way past Stroud to Nailsworth, along the route of a former railway branch line running between Stonehouse and Nailsworth. Sometimes referred to as the **Dudwell Donkey**, the line was completed in 1867 but rapidly ran into financial trouble, and was eventually closed in 1949, well before Beeching's Axe. The way is navigationally pretty straightforward, but if in doubt you should usually continue ahead on the wider path.

Riding along a very quiet road near Nympsfield

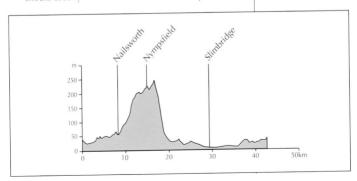

109

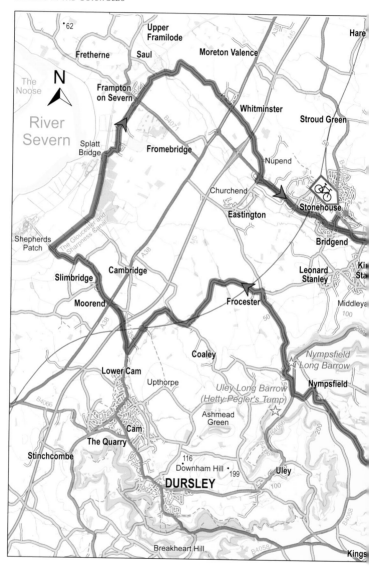

This cycle path first takes you along the right-hand pavement of the A419. Soon after a side-turning, the trail veers away from (but remains parallel to) the main road, rejoining this (heading right) shortly after a roundabout. At the next major junction (with Ryeford Road South), use a toucan crossing over the A419 and continue along its left-hand pavement. Cross an entrance to a small industrial yard; the cycle path now separates itself from the road with a small line of woodland.

Eventually rejoining the main road, the cycle path uses a third toucan crossing to return to the right-hand side of the A419 and then bypasses a roundabout.

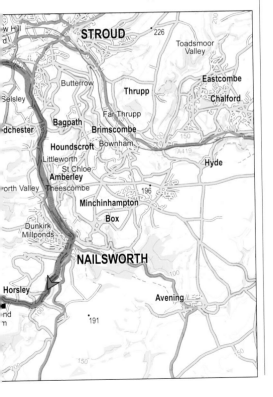

Continue towards Nailsworth through a corrugated iron-walled tunnel and then go straight ahead where a track bears left towards Stroud. Cross two dirt tracks, the second in a sudden dip where a rail bridge used to run. Where the track forks, stay left (on the wider path) and continue under a bridge.

Shortly after this the trail crosses three minor roads in quick succession and then runs close to the main road. The trail now briefly runs past a more industrial area and includes a short section of tarmac; shortly beyond this the trail runs past some old millponds below on the right.

> These are the **Dunkirk Millponds**, which improved the water supply to the 18th-century mills so much that they became the most productive in the county. They fell into disuse with the advent of steam (which used a nearby source of coal) but were restored in 2007–2008 as a wildlife wetland site.

Continue along the rail trail to reach an access road, bending left then right, then right again past the fire station. Turn left onto the A46 on the edge of **Nailsworth**. After 50m turn right at a roundabout and go up Spring Hill (now leaving NCN45). Almost immediately, turn left onto Old Market Road towards Newmarket. Continue to Cossack Square and turn left towards Shortwood by The Britannia PH. The road rises moderately steeply; at a junction where the major road becomes Pike Lane (and its gradient steepens noticeably), turn left onto the continuation of Horsley Lane, continuing more gently uphill.

At a T-junction turn right onto a busier road (B4058). Continue along this road for 3km, through the pretty, linear village of **Horsley**. The ascent is fairly relentless but never too steep, and it eases off completely by Nupend Farm, which also marks the start of the upland plateau.

Fork right to **Nympsfield**; the road now undulates to a T-junction. Turn right and descend to a junction by Barberi Cottage. Turn left and climb gently up this lane. Turn left at an oblique junction outside the Rose and Crown Inn; 50m later fork left and out of the village.

At a T-junction turn right, then cross the B4066 to Frocester. ▶ This wide country lane bends rightwards immediately after the junction and descends steeply (1:10) all the way to **Frocester**. At a crossroads by The George Inn turn left towards Coaley.

Cross a railway line; a short ascent is rewarded with a pleasant descent to a low bridge. Turn right at a T-junction towards Cam and Dursley, passing Cam and Dursley station on the way. At another T-junction turn right onto a main road (A4135) towards Gloucester. Cross bridges over the railway and motorway and descend to a large and awkward roundabout with the **A38**.

Cross this, now heading to **Slimbridge**. Continue all the way through this long village (joining NCN41) to the Patch Bridge canal swing bridge. ▶

Cross the bridge and immediately turn right along the towpath. Cross a farm access track by the next bridge, and at a third swing bridge (Splatt Bridge) cross back over the canal on a short access lane, passing a beautiful traditional tithe barn near the church. Turn left onto a country lane and stay on the major road as it bends right past the pretty Tythe House B&B. Turn left at a junction

A brief detour left here along the B4066 leads to Uley Long Barrow (Hetty Pegler's Tump) – an ancient burial mound dating from more than 5500 years ago.

Continuing on the road beyond this brings you to the Wildfowl and Wetlands Trust Centre at Slimbridge.

Early-morning calm waters near Patch Bridge on the Gloucester and Sharpness Canal

The old and picturesque tithe barn in Frampton on Severn

Frampton is notable for a very wide green, containing many wetland ponds, on either side of the main road towards the northeast end of the village.

The cycle path broadly follows the line of the A419, with occasional detours onto old sections of road and other parallel quiet roads.

just after a couple of timber-framed houses and continue through **Frampton on Severn** to reach a slightly staggered crossroads. ◄

Cross this onto Whitminster Lane (swapping signs for NCN41 with NCN45, which you can now follow all the way back to Stonehouse) and go over the river bridge. Go through **Whitminster** – another long village – and cross over a mini-roundabout.

At a junction with a dual carriageway (A38), cross into Grove Lane towards Westend. A flyover crosses the motorway; go straight ahead at a large and busy roundabout over the A419 towards Eastington.

Take the next left just before a bridge over the Cotswold Canal/Stroudwater Navigation; the cycle route initially runs parallel to the Stroudwater canal before briefly running beside the A419, continuing on an old bit of road. ◄

Pass a roundabout by a business park and cross the A419. A cut-through leads to a short section of quiet road; as this joins the A419 continue straight ahead on a new section of cycle path. Bypass a roundabout and turn left into Bristol Road towards Stonehouse. After another short stretch on the A419's pavement, take the next left up Regent Street to return to the start.

ROUTE 17

Stow Loop via Blockley

Start/Finish	War memorial outside the Kings Arms PH, Stow-on-the-Wold (SP 192 258)
Distance	35km (22 miles)
Total ascent/descent	635m
Grade	Challenging
Terrain	63% roads, 37% off-road
Refreshments	On route: several in Stow; Golden Ball Inn (Lower Swell); community café (Blockley – NB both this and Longborough close at 1.00pm on Sundays) Short detour: Fox Inn (Broadwell); Longborough community café
Parking	Fosseway car park, Stow (free)
Cycle hire	Bourton-on-the-Water, Moreton, Chipping Campden or TY Cycles (mobile)
Road bikes?	Not suitable
Connecting routes	Routes 4 and 22
Note	Includes two short sections where pushing the bike is highly likely. This is one of the toughest off-road routes in the book. The A-road sections are easier than they look on the map.

This hilly outing has one the highest percentages of off-road terrain of all the routes in the book. It's not a particularly long route, but you will probably find it quite challenging, particularly the section towards Donnington at the end.

With the Kings Arms to your left, go down Digbeth Street (one-way) to a sharp T-junction at a small green. Turn right, following the main road uphill to a traffic light-controlled junction by the Unicorn Hotel. Use the right-hand filter lane to dog-leg right then left across the A429 and enjoy a fantastic long descent into **Lower Swell**.

Pass the Golden Ball Inn and turn right by a war memorial in a grassy triangle towards Upper Swell, continuing straight ahead towards Guiting Power at the next (immediate) junction. This lane goes uphill, initially

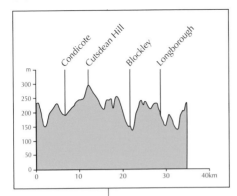

steeply, before reaching a crossing track marked 'unsuitable for motors' (easily missed).

Turn right onto this lovely stony track, crossing two major roads to gain a tarmac lane to **Condicote**. This twists and turns to reach a large oval village green (which acts as a roundabout). Take the next left off this towards Hinchwick.

Bend sharp left by Church View and continue straight ahead on an 'unsuitable for HGV' lane, where the major road bends right by a large new house (Cedar Gables). This lane soon becomes a stony track. At a junction with another country lane, turn right and rise up gently.

As the gradient eases, take a bridleway (Gloucester Way/GW) left into the woods. After 300m, at the edge of woodland, the GW turns left (do not exit the woods here on an inviting track straight ahead) and exits the

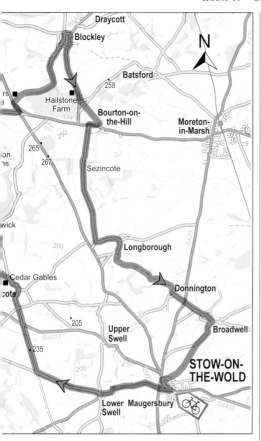

woodland roughly 50m later. It now follows the line of
a large hedge on your right. When you can see a hedge-
line marking the far end of the field about 100m ahead,
bear right through a gap in the hedge-line and onto a dirt
track. ▶

The next section passes over cultivated fields through
which the line of the right of way cuts – at first as a pair of
'tramlines' but becoming narrower and less clear further

Beware: this turn is
very easy to miss.

on. Initially head for a gap in a drystone wall 100m or so away. After passing through this maintain your line across the next field, heading towards the left edge of a conifer plantation roughly 600m ahead.

At the plantation follow a bridleway marker to cut across its left corner, very soon emerging onto a further large cultivated field. Continue this way, ultimately making for the far right corner of the field about 800m ahead. Pass through a gate, picking up a rough grassy track and going past a small area of woodland on your left. Gradually improving, the track continues up a long climb, eventually reaching the road at a crossroads (near Cutsdean).

Turn right towards Snowshill, then right again into a road that follows the edge of some woodland.

> Keep an eye out for an information panel at a rough layby. This marks the place where you can see a restored **ture**: a very rare Cotswolds-specific field layout, which enabled sheep to gain access to drinking water after large areas of land were enclosed into fields after the 1777 Enclosure Act.

To stay **on road**, stay on this road as it goes uphill and bends right towards the A424.

Where the road bends abruptly left and goes uphill, take a bridleway right. ◄ ◄ This follows the valley bottom into woodland and past old quarry workings. After 150m take a bridleway left, heading steeply up a side valley and out of the muddy woodland. Follow the left edge of a large field on a long climb up to a broad ridgeline (Bourton Downs) that's followed by a gentle descent.

The next 250m can be very muddy, rough and steep in places, but it doesn't last long so you should persevere.

As the track starts to descend more steeply (roughly 50m before a line of conifers comes in from the right), take a bridleway at the end of forestry on your left. This runs for nearly 1km through grassy fields; go along the left edge of the first field and then descend diagonally across the next, sloping to its far right-hand corner. The route now descends quite steeply over bumpy ground and turns left to reach the valley bottom, joining a tarmac road soon afterwards. ◄

On sections like this a small amount of speed helps, but not so much that you can't stop if necessary!

Turn right onto this, ascending steeply at first. After 1km you reach a crossroads on the hilltop with the busy

A424. Turn left towards Evesham and then keep left as this road joins another main road (A44) by a petrol station. Take a bridleway immediately opposite the petrol station (down the driveway of Troopers Lodge) and enjoy the descent on a mixed-surface track. ▶

The route emerges onto tarmac in **Blockley** and descends past The Crown Inn, the road soon becoming Bell Lane and passing the community café/shop. Ascend past the village green to a junction and turn right towards Draycott. Descend to another junction and turn right onto Lower Lane (B4479), which leads out of the village. This initially descends, but it soon ascends steeply, passing Hailstone Farm.

Close to the top of the hill a road turns left towards Batsford; ignore this, instead taking a rough bridleway bearing leftwards across a cultivated field (detour on the road to the next junction left if necessary) then crossing straight over a second minor road. Continue through a gate immediately opposite; the wide track soon narrows as it passes the left edge of a patch of woodland. After this ignore all side-turns and enjoy a fantastic, gentle

A restored ture on the route between Cutsdean and Blockley

This can be a little muddy and awkward in places.

The enjoyable (and easy) singletrack descent through wildflowers to the edge of Bourton-on-the-Hill

singletrack descent to a stony track. Turn right up this and go over an old cattle grid, turning right at the end onto a main road (A44) on the edge of Bourton-on-the-Hill.

Take the next left to Sezincote.

Sezincote House and Gardens (open Thursdays, Fridays and bank holiday Mondays, 2.00pm to 6.00pm) are very unusual, having been built in the style of a Rajasthani Palace in 1810 for Sir Charles Cockerell, who had come to love the style while working in India. Sezincote is reputed to have been the inspiration for the Brighton Pavilion.

Continue for roughly 3.3km, passing the entrance to the gardens before turning left for a short descent into **Longborough**.

Longborough is notable for a claim that the oldest confirmed specimen of **dinosaur**

(Metriacanthosaurus reynoldsi – 160 million years ago) was discovered in a nearby disused quarry.

Bend past the Coach and Horses PH and turn right beside the primary school towards Stow. Just past a red phone box fork left on a minor lane (this runs almost parallel to the main lane); pass a spring and go left onto a dead-end lane.

When the tarmac ends continue on a stony track between hedges to a gateway into newly- planted woodland. Keep to the right edge of this and pass beside more mature woodland. Persevere with a very steep and often boggy uphill section (this is likely to involve a push), then bend left at the top into the woodland on a much easier section of track. Another very short section of muddy track leads to grassy pasture. Cross this pasture diagonally rightwards and follow a line of individually fenced-in trees in the second field to its far right end. Now continue on the same line past the walled garden of a large manor house.

Exit left onto a tarmac lane on the edge of **Donnington**. Turn left by a restored barn, continuing to a junction with the A429. Follow the opposite lane to **Broadwell**, crossing a ford at the bottom of the descent. Turn right shortly after this, then left towards Stow.

At the top of a long straight climb, take a bridleway left immediately after a wide farm track entrance, initially running through woodland. This is the Monarchs Way, which regains tarmac on the edge of Stow by a few buildings. Continue on tarmac past a couple of springs. Turn right at a T-junction then left opposite the police station. Continue through the marketplace to return to your start point.

ROUTE 18

Burford Loop via Northleach

Start/Finish	Tourist Information Centre, Burford (SP 251 123) NB This is wrongly marked on many maps!
Distance	43km (27 miles)
Total ascent/descent	470m
Grade	Challenging
Terrain	79% roads, 21% off-road
Refreshments	On route: several in Burford (try Huffkins tea room); community shop/café (Coln St Aldwyns); several in Northleach; village tea shop (Sherborne); Fox Inn PH (Little Barrington) Short detour: New Inn (Coln St Aldwyns)
Parking	Guildenford car cark (back of Burford, free)
Cycle hire	Bourton-on-the-Water, Lechlade or TY Cycles (mobile)
Road bikes?	Yes, but diversions may be needed at Westwell and via Bibury/Ablington to avoid off-road sections.
Connecting routes	Routes 7, 12, 13 and 14
Note	Uses 200m of main road (A40) on the edge of Burford to link quiet roads together. Also contains some tricky off-road sections.

This enjoyable route visits two of the historic wool towns of the Cotswolds (Burford and Northleach), traverses part of a former Roman road, passes a medieval castle and has plenty of challenging bridleways. Oh, and it has a few hills too, but they're not as steep or high as the ones in the previous route!

Cross the High Street into Priory Lane. Follow this as it twists and turns past the former Wadworth Brewery. At a crossroads by the Lamb Inn go straight over into Tanners Lane, rising out of the village and to a busy main road (A40).

This crossing is awkward; it involves cycling along the main road for roughly 200m before turning left onto a lovely quiet single-track lane to

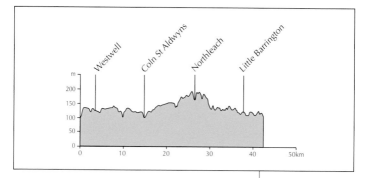

Westwell. This becomes very pleasantly tree-lined as you reach the edge of the village after roughly 2.5km. ▶ Turn left at a T-junction to Holwell and continue along another single-track lane to reach the hamlet.

Stay on the major road in **Holwell**, bending right past the war memorial and past a track (restricted byway) to Fox House. Immediately after the next house turn right onto a second restricted byway – initially waymarked as the d'Arcy Dalton Way (DD Way). ▶

Bend right (SP 231 087 – still on the restricted byway) where the DD Way continues straight ahead. As this ends, turn right then immediately right again onto a very narrow 'failed' road. You will be following the line of this for roughly 4.5km.

> This is **Akeman Street**, a former Roman road linking Watling Street (near St Albans) with the Fosse Way (near Cirencester). It is now a single-track lane with frequent potholes and encroaching grass.

Cross a country lane, now leaving any pretence of tarmac behind as the bridleway runs beside a couple of fields. Cross another country lane and go along the edge of a further field.

Just before a large metal gate (SP 202 074) the bridleway forks right, initially following a fainter vehicle track down a slight dip. (Ignore a footpath going through

To stay **on road**, continue straight on this road to join Akeman Street at the valley bottom.

It's very easy to take the first byway by mistake!

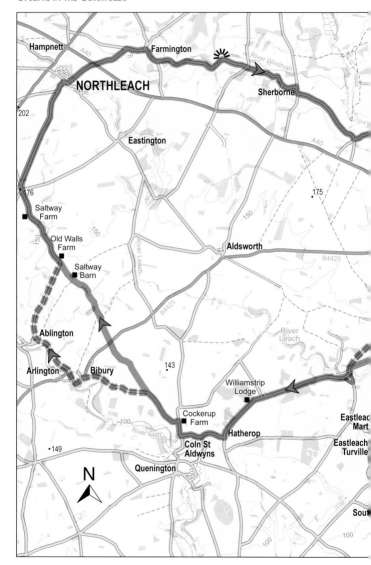

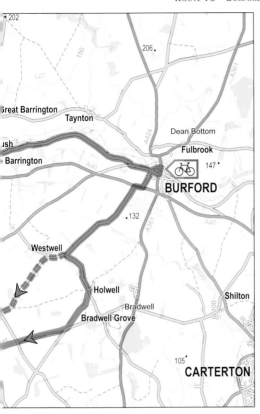

the gate.) In the dip, follow vehicle tracks left through a gap in the hedge and descend to cross a short boggy section. The rise on the far side to regain plateau-level is very steep. ▶ Continue straight ahead through a long field, then descend steeply (but briefly) on a stony track to a country lane.

Turn left onto this and drop down to the valley bottom. Ignore a Hatherop Estate track and take the next right to **Hatherop**, rising steeply at first. (For a gentler gradient take the following turn sharp right instead.)

The challenge is to complete this section without stopping or putting a foot down – it is possible in dry conditions!

125

The Hatherop Estate is now owned by the **Ernest Cook Trust**, which was founded by one of Thomas Cook's grandsons after he sold his share in the travel agency. Its aim is to preserve large estates and use them to help educate young children in a rural outdoor environment.

Continue on the major road for roughly 4km, bending left by Williamstrip Lodge. As you enter the village, turn right to **Coln St Aldwyns**.

In Coln St Aldwyns, continue past a conker tree in the middle of a junction by the community shop/café. Then, following signs towards Bibury, turn right. Continue out of town past **Cockerup Farm** and then turn left.

To stay **on road**, stay on this minor road to Bibury and Arlington (see map) and follow signs from there back north towards Northleach.

Descend slightly, ignoring a green-gated track entrance in the bottom of the dip. When the road next begins to dip down slightly, bear right onto a vehicle track (shortly before another set of green double wooden gates). ◀ Continue along this; after an initial moderate climb, which can get somewhat overgrown, the vehicle

Bridleway between fields near Bibury

track fades a bit into the edge of the field. Continue straight ahead into the next field, now following a wide grassy strip between crops.

At the end of this field (SP 131 072) continue through a metal gate and onto a partially rutted grassy track, which then forms a wide strip between crops. Bear slightly rightwards towards a lane (B4425). Cross this and continue straight ahead for roughly 1km down a much easier-going restricted byway.

Cross over a stony track (bridleway) and follow the field edge as it bears slightly left, going beside two further fields on an increasingly stony track. At a junction of tracks bend left then right. The main track is sometimes vague here: head towards a small brick building (Saltway Barn) then turn right on a clearer track.

The main track emerges on to a country lane at a sharp bend near Oldwalls Farm. Turn right onto this and continue for roughly 2.2km, with a sharp descent followed by a long gradual ascent to two minor crossroads in quick succession. Follow signs to **Northleach**, staying on the major road at the first and taking the second right. ▸ In Northleach bend past a school, then at a 'Stop' junction turn right onto Church Walk. Turn left at the next junction and continue straight ahead at a right-hand bend to reach the market square.

You also join NCN48 here.

Northleach gained its market charter in AD1227, becoming a major centre for the Cotswolds woollen industry between the 14th and 16th centuries. The substantial wealth generated from the export of raw wool was used to improve the town. It is said that there is a series of interconnected stone vaulted tunnels below many of the town houses and streets, but little is known of their origin.

From the market square turn right onto High Street, then turn first left (roughly 100m) into Farmington Road. Climb moderately steeply up this road, which becomes quite narrow as it leaves the village and goes under the A40. Turn right at a T-junction and into **Farmington**, now

An unusual octagonal stone building in Farmington, built for the Festival of Britain in 1951

The first was built for the Festival of Britain in 1951; the second is a former Victorian pump house on a village green triangle.

It's worth stopping briefly here as views of the Windrush are surprisingly fleeting and limited. This is the best one on the route.

following NCN47 (National Byway) signs all the way to Burford.

Pass a couple of unusual octagonal stone buildings in Farmington. ◄ Continue on the major road for roughly 3km to reach the outlying edge of **Sherborne village**.

Cross over a major road to the long, strung-out village 'centre', with a glimpse of the River Windrush just after Sherborne House (right) on a short but enjoyable descent. ◄ Pass the village tea room then continue on the major road to **Windrush**.

Turn right to **Little Barrington** (opposite The Fox Inn); bend right and go uphill past the unusual village meadow. Turn left to Burford on another lovely quiet country lane. Overall descending, this undulates for roughly 4km. At a T-junction turn left and into Burford, passing the Lamb Inn. Turn left onto the main street.

ROUTE 19
Stroud Loop via Chavenage House

Start/Finish	Stroud railway station, rear entrance (SO 849 051)
Distance	66km (41 miles)
Total ascent/descent	1000m
Grade	Challenging
Terrain	100% roads (two optional off-road detours)
Refreshments	On route: Fostons Ash Inn (nr Sheepscombe); The Highwayman Inn (nr Winstone by A417 junction – limited opening hours); several cafés/pubs in Tetbury, Nailsworth (try Scrumptious Café or Hobbs House Bakery in Nailsworth – NB Hobbs House closed on Sundays) and Stroud, Off-road detour: Butchers Arms PH (Sheepscombe)
Parking	Long stay car park on London Road (max 23hrs, fee)
Cycle hire	Stroud, Stonehouse, Painswick (for electric bikes) or Cheltenham
Road bikes?	Yes (off-road detours optional)
Connecting routes	Routes 16, 21 and 22
Note	This route is long and hilly, with major roads at the start. In wet conditions the optional bridleway through Workman's Wood (thick mud and steep gradient) may become extremely challenging; in such conditions it is best avoided.

Stroud is notoriously ill-designed for bicycles. This route avoids most of the struggle to exit against the one-way system/pedestrian streets, but the downside is a short flight of steps and some main roads. On the upside, this is the most scenic route out of Stroud, rising relatively gently (by Stroud standards!) to roughly follow the watershed of the Slad and Frome Valleys, returning via the easy-going Stroud Valley cycle track.

From the station car park turn right onto Cheapside. Go straight ahead over the first roundabout and turn right at the next one (first of a double mini-roundabout) to join the A46. (You follow this for roughly 800m to exit Stroud.)

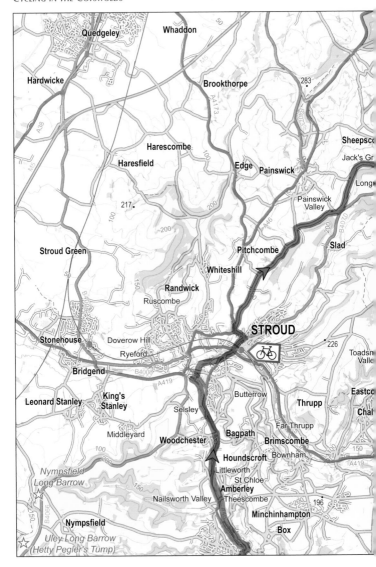

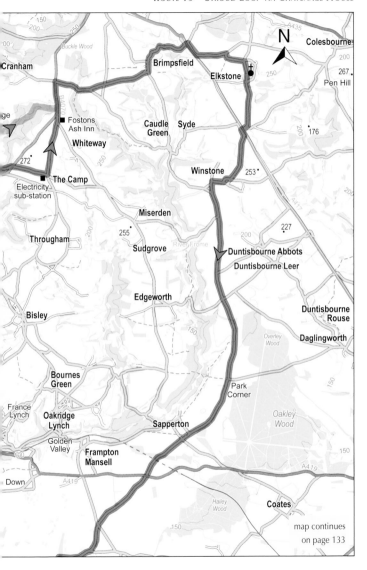

map continues
on page 133

131

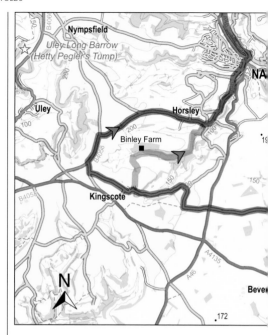

Unlike most Cotswold towns and villages, **Stroud** is a working town rather than one that has become completely dominated by the tourist trade. The Stroud area is sometimes referred to as the Golden

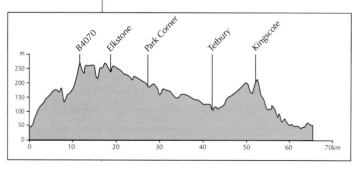

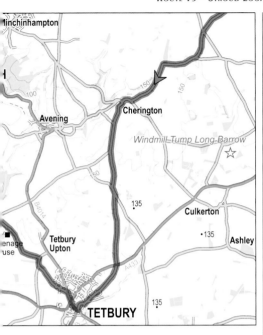

Valleys, relating to the great wealth generated by
the 150 or so 18th- and 19th-century woollen mills
that lined the five river valleys converging in Stroud.

Continue past the bus stands and turn left at the next
roundabout. Turn right (towards Painswick) at the following roundabout, then roughly 100m later turn right
onto Painswick Old Road (signposted to Wick Street) to
leave behind the busy A-roads. This initially steep lane
soon eases to a gentle and undulating climb. Continue
along the major road for roughly 4.5km, following signs
towards Bulls Cross and passing four junctions to the left.

At the fifth junction two roads join obliquely from
the left; take the second (11 o'clock) to follow a cut-
through avoiding the B-road at the top of the hill (Bulls
Cross), then go left again onto the descending road,

continuing into the hamlet of Longridge and onto the edge of **Sheepscombe**. Follow this for just over 3km, through a linear section of housing followed by a steep ascent over the final 550m to join a major road (B4070).

Cross the B4070 towards Miserden, and just after an electricity substation turn left at a major crossroads towards Birdlip. Stay on this busier road for nearly 2.5km. At a T-junction with the B4070, turn right (to continue cycling north ahead), passing the Fostons Ash Inn on your right.

The end of this trail is steep; in wet conditions the woodland trail may be unrideable.

Riding through Worksmans Wood in spring alongside wild garlic flowers

Off-road alternative: Workmans Wood

An optional detour turns left towards Sheepscombe village and across a steep-sided valley. ◄ Immediately before the Butchers Arms PH turn right onto a dead-end lane to Sheepscombe Far End. This undulates gently then becomes a bridleway as it enters Workman's Wood/ Ebworth Estate.

Take the right fork (don't go through a gate) onto a stony woodland track. Rise gently, ignoring a track forking right slightly below the main track. Descend briefly to

pass just left of a couple of lakes and then rise next to the line of the incoming stream. Bear right past a black corrugated tin shelter and rise progressively steeply to two large wooden gates at the upper edge of the woodland. ▶

Continue along a steep grassy trail and exit through gates to the road. Join the main road north towards Birdlip.

Take the next right to **Brimpsfield**, crossing a steep-sided valley, then continue left and then straight ahead at a major crossroads and into the village. Turn left at a T-junction towards Birdlip, and just after a red phone box turn right towards Cirencester. This twisty road crosses the headwaters of the River Frome and rises up under a dual carriageway (A417) flyover.

Turn right immediately after this flyover. Roughly 800m after a bend left, turn right onto a minor road.

At a major crossroads turn right towards Elkstone Church. The road eventually bends right and goes under the A417 again. Turn left at the T-junction immediately after this and continue into **Winstone**.

Turn left at a major crossroads towards Sapperton and follow this (ignoring all minor roads) for roughly 8km to pass close to the village of **Sapperton**.

Now follow signs for Cherington for roughly the next 6.5km. During this, go over a major crossroads leading to a pleasant dip and short re-ascent, then cross the A419 before contouring across a major road on a slightly oblique angle. At a T-junction on the edge of **Cherington** turn right towards Tetbury and bend left through the village. Continue on the major road for nearly 4.5km to the **A433**, crossing this with a slight dog-leg left then right onto Cirencester Road.

Continue all the way into **Tetbury** through a traffic-calmed area and up a hill into The Chipping. Continue along Chipping Street and turn right at the roundabout by The Snooty Fox PH onto Long Street. Where this bends sharp right on a junction take the second left towards Chavenage on the B4014. Continue past the entrance to the rugby ground and immediately after this fork left

In spring this woodland becomes a blue and white carpet of wild garlic flowers and bluebells.

into Chavenage Lane (do not follow the brown signs to Chavenage House).

Ignore all side turns before the entrance to Chavenage House.

> **Chavenage House** (open Thursdays and Sundays 2.00pm–5.00pm, May to October) is an unpretentious stately home with a lot of history. The earliest known owner was Princess Goda, sister of Edward the Confessor. Famous visitors include Oliver Cromwell, who stayed there briefly during the Civil War. The house is reputedly haunted by the ghost of Charles I.

Continue past this and through a tree-lined avenue in Chavenage Green, taking the left fork where the avenue splits and eventually reaching the A46.

The avenue of trees by Chavenage House

Cross this onto an access road to Hazelcote Farm, bending sharp right just in front of the farm. Turn left at the next junction (by a white trig point set in the wall) and descend past a few houses before climbing moderately steeply into **Kingscote**. Continue through the village, bending right past the church. Turn right towards 'The Windmill' as the road bends sharp left. Now turn right at two T-junctions to reach the B4058. Turn right along this and descend to Horsley.

Off-road alternative: Kingscote to Horsley

Turn right as you enter the village (towards **Binley Farm**), continuing ahead on a bridleway running over a private lane, then bend right then left on a deviation of the bridleway around farm buildings. Descend to rejoin the farm track.

Near the bottom of the valley turn right by a wooden marker in front of the farm houses (but don't cross the stream) and follow a track into pasture. After roughly 350m bear left onto a faint but quite wide grassy track and descend through a small gate into woodland. A narrow track soon becomes a vehicle track, which is a bit

Riding along a level section of track on the descent from Kingscote to Horsley

rough and steep in a couple of places on the descent to a junction of tracks (roughly 1km after entering the woodland). Continue straight ahead (don't cross the stream here), following bridleway markers. The track now undulates but overall descends gently to pass a few houses, then bends right and rises again to a few more houses at the edge of **Horsley**. Turn left as another tarmac lane rises from the right, then turn right and immediately right again to emerge onto the B4058.

Descend the B4058 from Horsley, moderately steeply at first, and as you pass the Nailsworth village sign (near Pike Cottage) turn left and go briefly uphill along Horsley Road. This then descends quite steeply to a T-junction; turn right and descend to a further T-junction by The Britannia PH. Turn right then bend left onto Old Market. At the end, turn right to reach a roundabout by a stone clock tower.

Turn left onto the A46 and use the filter lane to turn right by Egypt Mill. Follow this road as it bends left past the fire station and gently descend the valley to Stroud on a 'rail-trail' cycleway. The way is navigationally simple for the next 5km, but beware of occasional road/access track crossings.

Roughly 100m before a corrugated tin tunnel (SO 836 043), turn right to Stroud. Follow the cycle path through a residential area (bending right to cross a stream, then going straight ahead at road crossings) to a toucan crossing over a main road (A46). Use this, then haul the bike up a set of steps using a wheel-track on the right. ◄ Continue under a bridge. Roughly 120m after two bridges in quick succession, the tarmac does a sharp bend left and doubles back on itself to rise steeply up to a road (Rodborough Hill).

A cycle track continues on the pavement to the right (don't cross the road). Just before the road reaches a roundabout, bear right onto Wallbridge and go under a subway. Emerge onto a cut-off road near the Lockkeeper's Café. Turn right onto a dead-end lane at a roundabout (onto Cheapside) and head back to the station.

There is no access from the next road back onto the track if you're tempted to detour left via the main road.

ROUTE 20
Cheltenham Loop via Cleeve Hill

Start/Finish	Cheltenham Spa railway station (SO 932 220)
Distance	52km (32 miles)
Total ascent/descent	1010m
Grade	Challenging
Terrain	95% roads, 3.5% trails, 1.5% off-road
Refreshments	On route: Cuppa Coffee and Cake (Cheltenham Spa); The Apple Tree PH (Woodmancote); Corner Cupboard and White Hart inns (Winchcombe); Kings Head PH and Mill Inn (Withington) Short detour: several in Cheltenham; several in Winchcombe; Chedworth Roman Villa museum café (Yanworth); The Craven Arms (Brockhampton); Seven Springs Inn (Seven Springs)
Parking	Cheltenham Spa railway station (all-day parking, fee)
Cycle hire	Cheltenham, Stroud, Stonehouse or The Bike Works (delivery option)
Road bikes?	Yes, with a 1km detour to avoid the off-road byway near Seven Springs (using the A435).
Connecting routes	Routes 19 and 22 (for the very fit!)

This is a challenging route with two very steep and long hills near the start (Cleeve Hill near Cheltenham and near Sudeley Castle at Winchcombe). It then undulates across ridgelines and finally descend towards Cheltenham down a steep scarp slope with fine views.

From the station access, don't exit onto the road – instead turn left onto the Honeybourne Line cycle track (NCN41) some distance opposite the station building.

> The cycle track follows a former **railway line**, originally built by the Oxford Worcester and Wolverhampton (OWW) railway company (acquired and redeveloped by GWR), which ran from Birmingham via Stratford to Bristol and the South West and gave the GWR a competing route against its Midland Railway rival. After

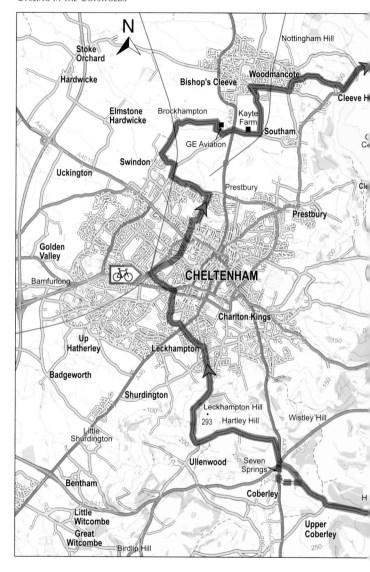

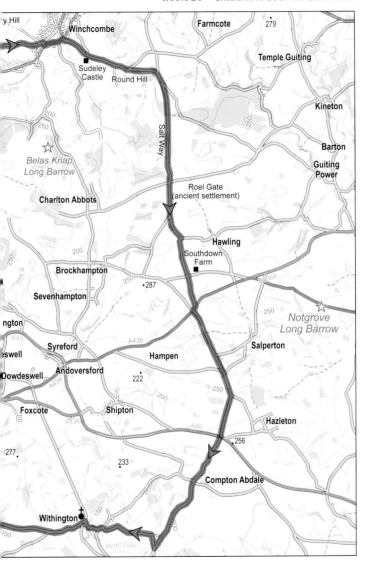

y_Hill

Winchcombe

Farmcote

· 279

Temple Guiting

A4632

Sudeley
Castle

Round Hill

ourne

Kineton

200

250

Salt Way

☆
*Belas Knap
Long Barrow*

Barton

**Guiting
Power**

Roel Gate
(ancient settlement)

Charlton Abbots

250

Hawling

Southdown
Farm

200

250

A4068

Brockhampton

· 287

Sevenhampton

250

☆
*Notgrove
Long Barrow*

ngton

A40

Syreford

Hampen

Salperton

eswell

A436

Dowdeswell

Andoversford

· 222

A436

200

250

Foxcote

A436

Shipton

A40

· 256

Hazleton

277 ·

· 233

Compton Abdale

✝
Withington ●

150

River Coln

250

200

141

Crossing Honeybourne Way, Cheltenham

nationalisation in 1948 the route initially attracted holidaymakers heading to Cornwall, then fell into decline. It was still used for freight, including fruit from the Vale of Evesham, until an accident near Winchcombe in 1976. Nowadays a short section north of Cheltenham Spa forms a useful cycleway out of town.

After roughly 1km fork left where the route divides under two bridges. Continue straight ahead over a junction of tracks by the Winston Churchill Memorial Gardens, and over a metal bridge.

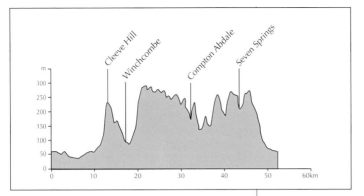

Turn right by a sports stadium then left onto Tommy Taylors Lane. Turn left at a mini-roundabout onto Swindon Lane and go over a mini-roundabout by Windyridge Road. Continue over a level crossing then turn right onto Wymans Lane. Turn left onto Church Road where Wymans Lane bends sharp right and goes under a railway bridge.

Turn right onto Quat Goose Lane then take the third right onto Brockhampton Lane. Continue over a level crossing and through **Brockhampton**. Bend a few times past GE Aviation and go left at a T-junction to rejoin the busy road (now Hyde Lane).

Go across an awkward junction with the **A435** (a cycle lane eventually appears between the filter lanes). Rise briefly up the hill; take the first left onto Kayte Lane (towards the cemetery) and follow its end in **Bishop's Cleeve**. Turn right onto Two Hedges Road and follow this past a school and over a railway bridge to a major crossroads. Turn left onto New Road.

As the road bends left at a small triangular green, turn right onto Stockwell Lane. ▶ The gradient is gentle at first but steepens progressively, particularly after Post Office Lane turns off to your right.

At the top of the hill turn left onto a main road (B4632). This rises gently and briefly to a golf course entrance. The road descends all the way into Winchcombe, but a

A steep hill warning sign (25%) is slightly hidden back from the junction, but the challenge now begins!

143

quieter, more undulating route leads off left after another 800m. Take this, and then turn right at a T-junction on a bend by the Corner Cupboard Inn. Go left onto the main road through **Winchcombe**.

Immediately before the White Hart Inn, turn right onto Castle Street. Follow this narrow lane out of the town and past the back entrance of Sudeley Castle. ◄ Now the second hill challenge begins! Continue up this lane (ignoring side-turns) to reach a broad ridgeline.

Fork right (towards another Brockhampton) then descend gently on this road for about 6km, passing over two minor crossroads after 2.7km (**Roel Gate**) and 5.3km (near **Southdown Farm**).

> This road runs along the course of one of many ancient **salt routes** from the Droitwich mines to the rest of England – in this case towards Lechlade to connect with barges on the River Thames.

At a junction with a main road (A436) turn right towards Cheltenham. After 100m (just beyond Cotswold Trailers) turn left onto a minor road. Follow this for nearly 4km to reach an awkward junction with the A40.

Cross straight over this, with care, onto a minor road (which involves bending left then right) to **Compton Abdale**. Enjoy a good descent then climb briefly to reach the start of this linear village before descending further. Continue ahead, crossing a major road (going past a crocodile spring on the other side). Continue into the village towards Roman Villa.

Rise over another short ridgeline then enjoy a good descent to a T-junction by a large grassy triangle.

> There are two former Roman villas near here: **Compton Abdale** is barely visible below the ridgeline you have just descended, but **Chedworth** (much better known, with a museum) is a 2km detour left from here.

Katherine Parr came to live here for the rest of her short life after surviving Henry VIII.

The pleasant valley of the River Coln near Withington

Turn right to **Withington** and descend into the village. Turn left at a T-junction and twist past the Mill Inn. At a crossroads by a church turn left towards Chedworth. Turn right towards Hilcot and rise up over another ridgeline.

As the gradient eases, fork right towards Hilcot. Ignore a tarmac track right, then descend quite steeply down a road in poor condition. ▸ Rise to cross over a more major lane onto a road marked 'unsuitable for HGV'. This continues uphill, steeply at first. After 1.6km (from Hilcot) you'll pass a side-turn towards Upper Coberley.

There is a bridleway 200m further on but this is not the one you want.

Roughly 800m after the Upper Coberley turning, take a restricted byway (dirt track) to the right. ▸ This descends, steeply in places, over a somewhat rough surface to emerge between roundabouts by the **A435** at **Seven Springs**. A careful choice of line gives a smooth descent for much of the way. ▸

Following prolonged wet weather there is potential for flooding in the dip at the bottom.

To stay **on road**, bear left then right on the A435 to Seven Springs.

This track may be difficult in wet conditions, and even in the dry may be difficult if you're not used to off-roading.

There are excellent views over the Cheltenham valley from the steep scarp slope along this road.

Use a toucan crossing to avoid the busy main roads, then turn right onto an access track which joins a quiet lane (Hartley Lane) running just left of the A435. Follow this over a gentle hill and eventually down to a T-junction; turn right along **Leckhampton Hill**. ◄ Descend into a much more urban area. Go straight ahead at a pair of mini-roundabouts (using the right-hand lane at the first). Pass some traffic lights then turn left almost immediately into Moorend Road. Bend right and go over a mini-roundabout.

Continue ahead at a traffic light-controlled cross-roads and turn left at a mini-roundabout. Follow this as it bends around the green park, turning left onto St Stephen's Road at the next mini-roundabout. Just before a busy junction with a main road (A40), turn left, following signs for 'Lansdown cycle route to Queens Road' (this uses the pavement), and go over a toucan crossing. Follow a minor road on the far side (Queens Road), pass a traffic light-controlled crossroads and return to the station.

ROUTE 21
Malmesbury Loop via Tetbury

Start/Finish	Market Cross, Malmesbury (ST 933 872)
Distance	48km (30 miles)
Total ascent/descent	430m
Grade	Challenging
Terrain	75% roads, 25% off-road
Refreshments	On route: several in Malmesbury and Tetbury; The Horse Guards PH (Brokenborough); The Royal Oak PH (Leighterton); Star Inn PH (Hullavington) Short detour: The Kings Arms (Didmarton); The Neeld Arms (Grittleton); The Wheatsheaf PH (Corston)
Parking	Station Road (on the Gloucester Road Ind Est – closed for carnival last week of August; fee)
Cycle hire	Cheltenham, Stroud, Stonehouse, Chippenham, Somerford Keynes or The Bike Works (delivery option)
Road bikes?	Not suitable
Connecting routes	Routes 15 and 19 (for the very fit!)
Note	Although not particularly long, this is the toughest route in the book due to its off-road sections and perhaps stretches the bounds of 'non-technical' off-road riding, with a very small rocky step on the bridleway near Beverston and a technical dip and re-ascent in Dunley Wood. However, as both difficulties are very short-lived the effort is worthwhile (even if it's necessary to walk a short distance with the bike). NB Novices who are unsure about off-road riding should not attempt this before gaining confidence on easier routes, or in anything other than ideal conditions. Nearly everyone else should also avoid it in wet conditions!

This route has it all: challenging off-road sections and easier bridleways, country lanes, several pubs en-route, haunted mansions and even flying monks! The off-road terrain is quite tough so please read the special note, particularly if you're new to off-road riding.

Facing away from The Whole Hog restaurant, turn right onto Oxford Street and bend sharply right around the abbey.

147

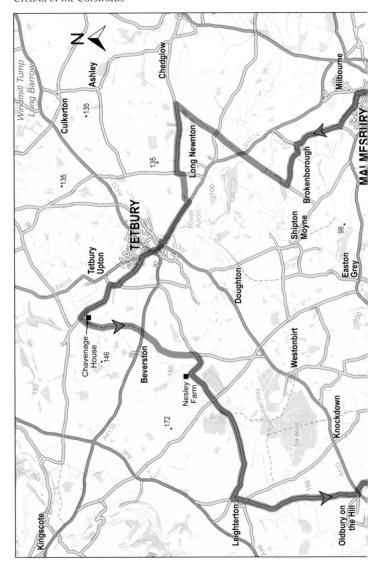

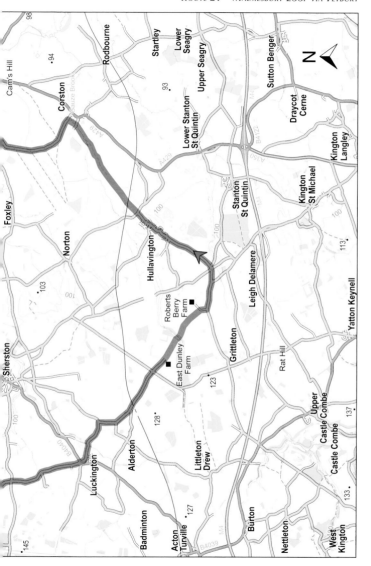

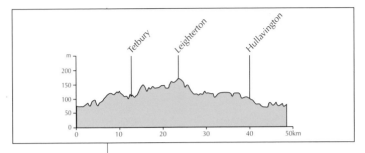

Malmesbury Abbey – where an 11th-century monk attempted one of the earliest recorded efforts at human-powered flight

Malmesbury Abbey was founded as a monastery in AD675 by Maidulph (the 'Black Prince' – whose name is thought to be a reference to his being a black-robed Benedictine Monk with royal connections) and is the burial site of King Aethelstan, the first King of England. The current part-ruined building dates from the 12th century. Strangely enough, the Abbey is also notable for hosting the first recorded human flight: in AD1010 a monk called Eilmer, having studied the Greek fable of Daedalus, created a primitive glider and flew 200m from the abbey roof.

Turn right at a T-junction at 'The Triangle' and pass The Three Cups PH. Continue downhill on Gloucester Road and turn left towards Park Road Industrial Estate at a mini-roundabout.

As the road bends slightly left and becomes Old Alexander Road, turn right to stay on Park Road. At a T-junction turn right, cross over a small stream bridge and head up a gentle hill into **Brokenborough**. Take the second dead-end lane on the left and cross the valley bottom.

At a junction with a large hedge straight ahead, turn right onto the **Fosse Way** (following byway signs for nearly 4km, but beware of numerous farm track crossings and a few gates over this). Pass left of a ford on an arched stone bridge. ▶ Then cross a country lane. At a second road junction, cross with a slight dog-leg left then right. Fork left to avoid an old disused airfield access.

Regaining tarmac, turn sharp left, almost back on yourself. At a T-junction turn left towards **Long Newnton**. Turn right opposite a church onto a bridleway/green lane. By a small wooden gate (directly ahead) bend abruptly left – this last short section often gets somewhat overgrown.

Turn right onto the road (B4014) and continue into **Tetbury**. Rise up into the town, bending left then right past The Snooty Fox to reach a roundabout by the market-place. Continue straight ahead onto Long Street. Where this bends sharp right on a junction, take the second left towards Chavenage on the B4014. Continue past the entrance to the rugby ground and immediately after this fork left into Chavenage Lane (not following the brown signs to Chavenage House).

Ignore all side turns before the entrance to **Chavenage House** (open Thursdays and Sundays 2.00pm–5.00pm, May to October).

Roughly 400m later, turn left onto a bridleway (Macmillan Way), passing a large green corrugated tin barn. Continue down a rutted grassy track and beside a field. ▶ Continue into a grassy meadow, bending slightly left then right to continue roughly straight ahead. At the top of this field continue on a dirt track.

The ford is rarely rideable, even in dry conditions, due to a couple of deep pools in the track either side of it.

This gets quite steep and rooty in places and there is a very short section of rocky step on the steepest part of the descent, but if you need to dismount it doesn't last long.

If tempted to divert through Westonbirt, bear in mind that the hoof-holed bridleways rarely dry out – even in summer!

At a main road (A4135) take a dog-leg right then left onto the continuation Macmillan Way (now a byway). The track briefly becomes rough, damp and moderately steep. At a junction with a lane, turn right then right again (unsigned, **not** towards Westonbirt). Bend left by **Nesley Farm** and head towards Leighterton at a major crossroads. ◀

In **Leighterton** turn left by The Royal Oak onto The Street, towards Knockdown. Go past a church and duck-pond and towards Didmarton at a major crossroads. Take a dog-leg left then right across the A433, following signs to Sopworth.

Continue through **Sopworth**, heading towards Luckington at a minor crossroads. In **Luckington** follow signs towards Alderton; go straight ahead at a major crossroads, past a green corrugated tin Methodist church, a grassy triangle and a village church, and continue through a valley bottom. Turn right and stay on the major road to a crossroads. ◀ Cross over onto a dead-end lane to **East Dunley**. Cross over a farm track and continue ahead and into woodland. The track changes character completely here, crossing a short technical (and steep) descent and re-ascent on loose, flat rocks. ◀ On the far side it becomes a much friendlier grassy track, leading to the driveway to **Roberts Berry Farm**. Turn right onto this and then left onto a country lane.

This is another section of Fosse Way (Wiltshire Cycleway).

This section is only short but it is technical mountain biking.

Bend left and go through **Hullavington** past the Star Inn PH. At the far end of the village, pass a school and dog-leg left then right over a major crossroads and along the access track to Court Farm (no through road). Go under a railway bridge and past the farm to reach a ford. ◀ If so, use a short bridge (sometimes overgrown) to the left.

This is usually rideable in dry conditions, but after prolonged heavy rain it can be surprisingly deep.

Ignore a side-track left (ST 909 833), and when your track ends continue just left of straight ahead, along a grassy strip between two long fields. (Don't turn right to go past a roped section.)

Turn left at the end of these fields (ST 914 836). Bend right at the corner, and roughly 400m later go through the smaller of two gates in the fence on your left.

The unexpected ford at a tributary of the Gauze Brook near Hullavington can get surprisingly deep after prolonged wet conditions – here it's relatively low

From here (ST 917 838) continue along the right-hand edge of the field. Follow a slight narrowing into the next field and then a small muddy path sneaks down to the river and crosses it on a concrete bridge. Bend right after this, exiting via a gravel driveway on the edge of **Corston**.

Turn right onto a country lane and about 10m later turn left, almost back on yourself, and go up a dirt track. This soon leads to a lovely green lane. ▶ At the end of this, turn left onto a country lane and continue for roughly 3.3km to reach a sharply-angled T-junction with Foxley Road. Turn right (now on NCN254) and enter Malmesbury. Turn right at a T-junction then right again at the war memorial. Follow this to return to Malmesbury Abbey and the market cross.

On your right is Corston Quarry and Pond Nature Reserve.

ROUTE 22

Around the Cotswolds

Start/Finish	Stroud
Distance	209km (130 miles)
Total ascent/descent	3100m
Grade	Moderate to Challenging
Parking	Long stay parking is always likely to be an issue on a multi-day route. Despite the difficulties of transporting cycles by train, this is usually a better option – Stroud and Moreton-in-Marsh stations being the most convenient. There are, however, a few free car parks (unlimited stay) partway along the route: Old Rail Yard, Tetbury (best for people starting from Stroud); Queen Street, Cirencester; and Fosseway, Stow on the Wold. Or you could use the train to reach Cheltenham, Kemble or Evesham and cycle to the nearest point on the route. Alternatively, start at any other point – the trail passes many rural and town-edge locations where you can park safely without inconvenience to residents.
Accommodation	See individual days. Only a featured B&B and anything else marked with an asterisk is an endorsement; anything else is just a guide to what's available nearby. For campsites, 'CS' means it is a Camping and Caravanning Club Certified Site (you will need to be a member of the club to pitch up, but this can usually be sorted easily on-site).
Road bikes?	Yes. The route follows roads unless doing so would require the use of an A-road, in which case the main route goes off-road (with a road detour shown on the relevant map). Off-road detours make the route more interesting for those on suitable bikes; suggestions include Sheepscombe (Day 1), Bourton to Great Barrington (Day 3) and Kingscote to Horsley (Day 4).

This is a multi-day challenge visiting a wide variety of the key Cotswolds attractions in four gentle- or moderately-paced days. The toughest day is at the beginning and the toughest hill is at the start of the second day, but the prevailing winds should be helpful. Although Day 3 is significantly longer than the others its easier terrain means it feels less tough than the first two days, and Day 4 is probably the easiest of all. Experienced cycle tourists may well wish to compress Days 2 and 3 into one long day.

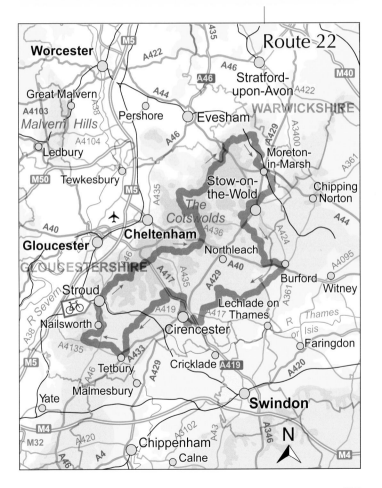

DAY 1
Stroud to Winchcombe

Start	Stroud railway station (back entrance onto Cheapside, SO 849 051)
Finish	War memorial, Winchcombe (SP 024 283)
Distance	47km (29 miles)
Total ascent/descent	1040m/1005m
Grade	Challenging
Terrain	100% roads (optional mountain-biking detour near Sheepscombe)
Refreshments	On route: Fostons Ash Inn (Calf Way); The Mill Inn PH (Withington) Short detour: Butchers Arms PH (Sheepscombe village); The Kings Head (Withington); The Craven Arms (Brockhampton); several in Winchcombe
Accommodation	Winchcombe is a large enough place to have a variety of options, although few are cheap. Try the Lion Inn on North Street: a friendly pub with a restaurant, clean, comfortable rooms and a great courtyard. The restaurant serves an excellent mid-priced range of dishes (if you can resist the bitter chocolate and passion fruit tart with sorbet after the day's hills you're made of sterner stuff than me!). For campers, the *site at Alderton (CS, 5km north of Winchcombe) is a pleasant and well-run site with very helpful owners.
Note	Uses main roads at the start to escape from Stroud.

This is the toughest day of the trip, with plenty of ascent to remind you that the Cotswolds are a range of hills – something many people forget until they encounter them on a bicycle! Particularly steep are the early one on Painswick Old Road and the one at the end of the Sheepscombe road, and then there's the low-rolling but sometimes surprisingly steep nature of the terrain as it crosses the grain of the landscape between Brimpsfield and Compton Abdale.

From the station car park turn right onto Cheapside. Go straight ahead over the first roundabout and then turn

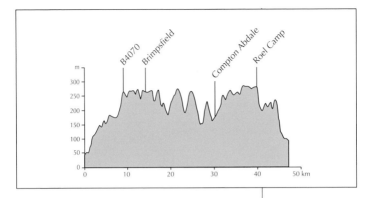

right at the next one (first of a double mini-roundabout) to join the A46. (You follow this for roughly 800m to exit Stroud.)

Continue past the bus stands and turn left at the next roundabout. Turn right (towards Painswick) at the following roundabout, then roughly 100m after this turn right onto Painswick Old Road (signposted to Wick Street) to leave behind the busy A-roads. This initially steep lane soon eases to a gentle and undulating climb. Continue along here for roughly 4.5km, following signs towards Bulls Cross and passing four junctions to the left.

> **Painswick** (on the far side of the valley) is regarded as one of several 'prettiest villages' in the Cotswolds. It would be worth a detour if it weren't for the brutally steep slopes, which, from Stroud, can only be avoided by the A46. However, there are great views across the valley to Painswick from this lane.

At the fifth junction two roads join obliquely from the left; take the second (11 o'clock) to follow a cut-through avoiding the B-road at the top of the hill (Bulls Cross), then go left again onto the descending road, continuing into the hamlet of **Longridge** and onto the edge of **Sheepscombe**. Follow this for just over 3km, through a

An ancient milestone near Stroud

157

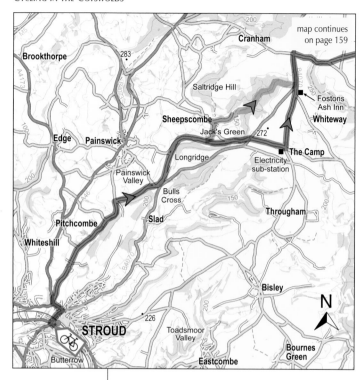

map continues on page 159

An optional off-road detour near here is described in Route 19, but this is best done with a light load as it is very steep. It also requires dry conditions!

linear section of housing followed by a steep ascent over the final 550m to join a major road (B4070). ◄

Cross the B4070 towards Miserden, and just after an electricity substation turn left at a major crossroads towards Birdlip. Stay on this busier road for nearly 2.5km then turn right at a T-junction by Fostons Ash Inn. Take the next right to **Brimpsfield**, crossing a steep-sided valley, then continue left and go straight ahead at a major crossroads and into the village. Turn left at a T-junction towards Birdlip, then just after a red phone box turn right towards Cirencester. This twisty road crosses the headwaters of the River Frome and rises up under a dual carriageway (A417) flyover.

Continue straight ahead and descend steeply to cross a valley. The way now undulates gently before descending once more into **Cowley**. Turn right at a T-junction and stay on the major road as it twists through the village. Cross over a main road (A435) and onto a single-track lane that rises up to the hamlet of **Upper Coberley**. At a T-junction by a grassy strip, turn right towards Hilcot and eventually descend steeply to a crossroads.

Continue over this towards Withington; a short descent soon leads to a long ascent on a roughly-surfaced road up the far side of the valley. ▶ Continue ahead at an unsigned junction with a tarmac lane, then turn left at an oblique junction. Follow this on a good descent into

The dip sometimes floods after prolonged wet weather.

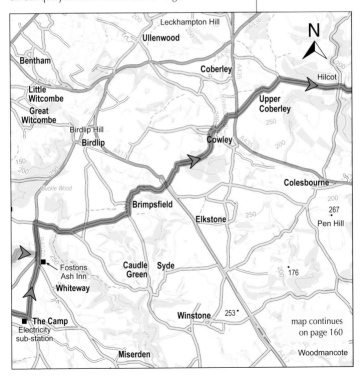

map continues on page 160

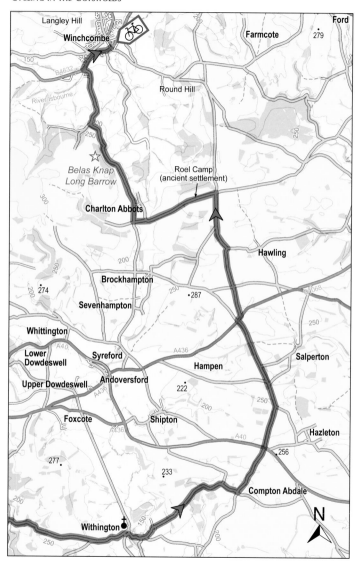

Langley Hill
Winchcombe
Ford
Farmcote
279
150
B4632
River Isbourne
Round Hill
200
250
Belas Knap
Long Barrow
300
Roel Camp
(ancient settlement)
Charlton Abbots
Hawling
200
250
Brockhampton
274
250
287
200
Sevenhampton
A4068
Whittington
250
Lower
Dowdeswell
A40
Syreford
Hampen
Salperton
Upper Dowdeswell
Andoversford
A436
222
A436
250
Foxcote
A436
Shipton
200
A40
Hazleton
277
250
256
233
Compton Abdale
200
Withington
150
250
N

Withington. In the village, follow signs to 'Roman Villa', first turning left (to effectively continue straight ahead) then turning right by the church and descending past the Mill Inn PH. The lane now rises over a steep hill before descending to reach **Compton Abdale**, some 3km distant.

It's worth looking out for a spring flowing from the mouth of a **stone crocodile** by the village crossroads. Although the current incarnation is new, the former version was in the village for over 100 years, and was eventually replaced when children had knocked most of its teeth out!

Turn left at the staggered crossroads and go up another steep hill to reach an awkward junction with the **A40**. Cross over this and stay on the major road (which now gently undulates) for nearly 4km to reach a crossroads with the **A436**.

Turn right towards Stow, and in roughly 100m turn left towards Hawling. Ignore all side-turns for just over 3km and then turn left towards **Charlton Abbots**. The road passes the site of an Iron Age settlement (Roel Camp, not obviously visible on the ground) then descends, steeply at first, for more than 1km. Rise gently up the far side to a crossroads and turn right to Winchcombe.

This road undulates gently for nearly 3km (and passes below Belas Knap) before bending sharp right and going

Dents Terrace – one of the prettiest rows in Winchcombe

steeply downhill into **Winchcombe**. Turn right (twice) at a T-junction at the bottom onto the B4632. The day's route ends by the war memorial in the centre of Winchcombe. (Continue beyond this and turn left into North Street to get to The Lion Inn.)

> In the 8th century King Offa (of Mercia, more famously the ruler who ordered a dyke to be built on the borders of Wales) founded an **abbey** at Winchcombe, at the crossroads of several important routes. Virtually nothing now remains of this abbey, unlike the remains of its nearest rival Hailes, just a few kilometres away.

DAY 2
Winchcombe to Stow-on-the-Wold

Start	War memorial, Winchcombe (SP 024 283)
Finish	Market Square, Stow-on-the-Wold (SP 192 258)
Distance	46km (29 miles)
Total ascent/descent	790m/650m
Grade	Challenging
Terrain	98% roads, 2% off-road
Refreshments	On route: Snowshill Lavender café (summer only); Morris and Brown café (Broadway Tower); Ebrington Arms (Ebrington); Fox Inn (Broadwell) Short detour: Snowshill Arms PH, Churchill Arms (Paxford); several in Winchcombe/Chipping Campden/Moreton-in-Marsh/Stow
Accommodation	The route nominally stops at Stow-on-the-Wold, but accommodation is available in plenty of towns and villages on the way, with Moreton, Stow, Bourton and Burford all being useful centres. The Old Stocks Inn on the marketplace at Stow-on-the-Wold is a great café stop, and they also have good value rooms. For campers/budget accommodation there is a rare Cotswolds YHA in Stow, and plenty of campsites between Moreton and Burford – try Ashspring House*, Great Rissington (CS) for a small and very peaceful site.
Note	There's a particularly steep hill at the start of this route, and A-roads are used in Moreton. Depending on the amount of daily cycling you prefer and the amount of sightseeing stops you wish to make en-route, you may choose to compress Days 2 and 3 into one day.

Today's route is of a similar length to yesterday's, but it's a little less hilly – although the start may have you thinking otherwise! It's a very steep ascent out of Winchcombe, but the views from the plateau and Broadway Tower are worth it. This is followed by a descent into the arts and crafts village of Chipping Campden, after which the terrain becomes more gently rolling, going past some of the must-see villages in the northern Cotswolds.

Look back to your left near the top of this to see how much you've climbed since Winchcombe.

From the war memorial continue W into the village on High Street. Take a narrow lane (Castle Hill – hard to spot in this direction) just before the White Hart Inn. Descend, initially, to cross the River Isbourne, after which a very steep and sustained hill (the 'Col du Sudeley', as a local wag has signposted it) rises for roughly 2km, passing the back of Sudeley Castle. As the gradient eases briefly, fork left towards Ford. This rises for just under a further 1km to Sudeley Hill. ◀ The route then gently descends to a col above the Hailes Abbey valley. Stay on this road for nearly 3km further as it undulates to reach a junction with the B4077 near Ford.

Cross over this and take the next left towards Snowshill. This now stays roughly at plateau-level to Chipping Campden. For now, continue for about 3.5km, passing through the hamlet of Taddington and ignoring

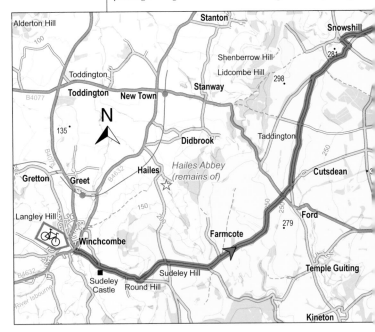

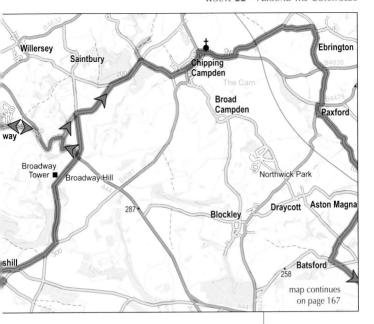

all minor roads until you reach a side-turn left to the pretty village of **Snowshill**.

Unless you need a pub stop, continue on the major road for a further 600m to a major crossroads. Ignore a

In summer the fields near Snowshill are turned an amazing shade of purple by a commercial lavender crop

165

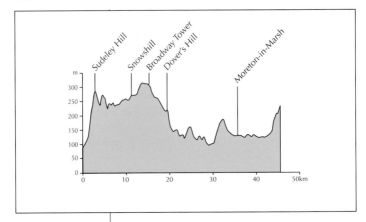

'Cotswold Lavender' sign straight ahead and turn left. Take the next right (also signed for Cotswold Lavender); this way takes a very slight detour in return for the best view of the lavender fields.

> In late June/early July the fields along this and the next section of road can be bright purple with a crop of **lavender**. But don't leave it too late in the year – as it's a commercial crop it is cut at its peak of flowering.

Take the next left, pass the café/lavender showfield and then turn left at a T-junction towards Broadway. As the road bends right, turn left towards Broadway Tower.

> **Broadway Tower** is a Gothic folly, built in 1799 for Lady Coventry as a (rather lavish!) experiment to see if a beacon fire could be seen on this hill from her home near Worcester. (It could.) You can see several counties from the top, and on a fine day the views stretch up to 62 miles distant. The hill is the second highest point in the Cotswolds after Cleeve Hill (Route 20).

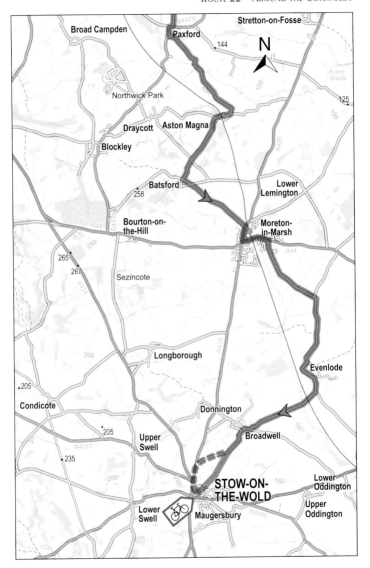

Views from Broadway Tower (entrance on foot) make the climb from Winchcombe worthwhile

Continue past the tower to a junction with the **A44**; go across towards Saintbury and stay on the major road past two junctions to the left.

Detour to Broadway

To visit Broadway village take the first turn left to descend on the A44. This descent is OK for experienced cyclists to use, although extreme care should be taken at the hidden turn-off left onto a cycle track leading to the Upper High Street partway down, as fast-moving vehicles will not expect you to stop suddenly for this. In ascent, the cycle path along the pavement of the A44 is clearly marked at the start, but turn left onto the road marked 'Farncombe Estate' to avoid the upper section of A44.

Detour to Dover's Hill

Take the third left turn towards Dover's Hill; just before the road begins to descend steeply, turn right onto a bridleway (access track) to Dover's Hill.

Dover's Hill is the site for the **Cotswold Olimpicks**, held annually in May. This event has been going for over 400 years and as such is locally regarded as the 'true' reviver of the modern Olympic Games.

Enjoy the view over this natural amphitheatre, then retrace your path back to the crossroads.

Continue straight ahead over the crossroads, descending steeply to **Chipping Campden**. Continue on the major road all the way through the town, passing a 'No Entry' road on the right towards the far end.

Another historically rich wool town of the Cotswolds, Chipping Campden became known as a centre for the **Arts and Crafts movement** when Charles Robert Ashbee moved there with his School of Arts and Crafts in the early 20th century. His mill buildings on Sheep Street are still used as craft workshops.

Chipping Campden is one of the many Cotswold towns made wealthy by the wool trade

Take the next right (Cider Mill Lane) towards Ebrington and turn left by the church. Pass a medieval banqueting hall/folly on the way out of town, then turn left to Ebrington and descend over a level crossing. The road now undulates all the way to this pretty, off-the-beaten-track village. Continue on the major road through the village and turn right towards Charingworth. By the Ebrington Arms turn right towards Paxford. Descend to a crossroads then continue uphill to a T-junction on the edge of **Paxford**.

169

Turn right and into the village; at a sharp bend right take a left turn towards Aston Magna. Take the next left by a small stone building, heading along a lovely quiet lane to the edge of **Aston Magna**. Turn right at the cross-roads and head steeply uphill, crossing over a railway bridge. Take the next left to Moreton-in-Marsh, still continuing uphill; the gradient finally eases as you exit the village. Eventually the road bends sharp left on the edge of **Batsford village**; descend on this road to **Moreton-in-Marsh**. Turn right onto the High Street (A429) and continue to a double roundabout by the marketplace (by the Black Bear PH).

Turn left onto the A44 towards Oxford and cross over the railway bridge. About 750m from the High Street turn right to Evenlode. Ignore all side-turns for roughly 7km, passing through **Evenlode** after roughly 4km. At a T-junction by a large stone barn on the edge of **Broadwell**, turn right towards Stow-on-the-Wold and then left shortly before a ford. Turn left again by a large village green and head uphill for 700m.

Immediately beyond a wide concrete farm-track entrance, turn left onto a restricted byway, initially running through woodland. ◄ This is the Monarchs Way, which regains tarmac on the edge of **Stow-on-the-Wold** by a few buildings. Continue on tarmac, turning right at a T-junction by a doctors surgery, left opposite the police station, and along to the market square.

To stay **on road**, continue along the road, then turn left onto the A429 to Stow-on-the-Wold.

DAY 3
Stow-on-the-Wold to Cirencester

Start	Market Square, Stow-on-the-Wold (SP 192 258)
Finish	Market Place, Cirencester (SP 023 020)
Distance	63km (39 miles)
Total ascent/descent	610m/720m
Grade	Moderate
Terrain	99% roads, 1% off-road
Refreshments	On route: Golden Ball Inn* (Lower Swell); Slaughters Country Inn (Lower Slaughter); Lamb Inn (Great Rissington); Fox Inn (Little Barrington); community café (Coln St Aldwyns) Short detour: New Inn (Coln St Aldwyns); several in Bourton/Burford/Bibury/Cirencester
Accommodation	Although there's plenty of accommodation in Cirencester, it's neither cheap nor always cycle-friendly. Try the Old Brewhouse on London Road – it's just a few minutes' walk from the centre but far enough away from any noise at night. The rooms are comfortable and there's a great courtyard to unwind in after the day's ride. Cycle storage is surprising but good; breakfast is excellent and there's plenty of choice for dinner in Cirencester. Campsites include Mayfield Park in Perrotts Brook (5km north of Cirencester) and Go-By-Cycle in Somerford Keynes (CS, 7km south of Cirencester – see Route 8 map).
Note	The route briefly uses two major roads (and crosses others); there are optional bridleways.

Today is a much easier-going day, despite being the longest of the trip. Traversing over rolling countryside, the hills are smaller and less steep-sided, and there are a few sections of optional off-road. Several times you will be following the line of a watershed before dropping down to cross a valley, eventually ending up in the former Roman metropolis of Corinium (Cirencester).

Head SE from the market square, past the Kings Arms and down Digbeth Street (one-way) to a sharp T-junction at a small green. Turn right and follow the main road uphill to the traffic lights by the Unicorn Hotel. Use the right-hand

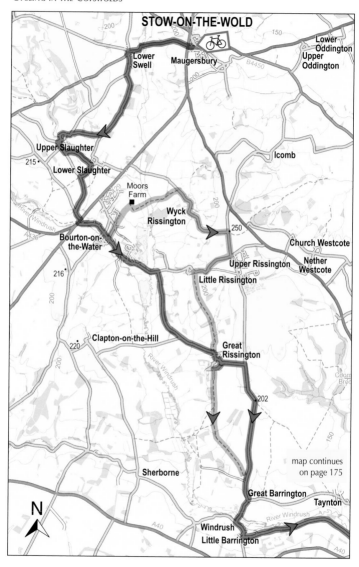

STOW-ON-THE-WOLD

Lower Swell

Maugersbury

Lower Oddington
Upper Oddington

Upper Slaughter

Lower Slaughter

Icomb

Moors Farm

Wyck Rissington

Bourton-on-the-Water

Church Westcote

Nether Westcote

Upper Rissington

Little Rissington

Clapton-on-the-Hill

Great Rissington

Sherborne

map continues on page 175

Great Barrington

Taynton

Windrush
Little Barrington

N

filter lane to dog-leg right then left across the main road (onto the B4068, unsigned) and enjoy a fantastic long descent into **Lower Swell**.

Pass the Golden Ball Inn and follow the major road as it bends left past a junction at the war memorial. Take the next left towards The Slaughters, staying on the major road until you reach a junction on a bend by South Lodge. Turn right here to **Upper Slaughter** and continue to a T-junction. Turn left and descend into the village. As the road levels out and bends left by a bridge, detour right to see the ford. ▸ Cross the ford and head steeply uphill, then turn right to rejoin the previous road, still heading uphill, and reach a T-junction.

Turn left to **Lower Slaughter** and stay on the major road to descend to this even prettier village opposite an old mill (easily missed). ▸ Take the first road right (next to Kingswell Cottage) and go uphill to a T-junction. Turn left towards Bourton-on-the-Water and then left again at a junction opposite a wall decorated with integral stone millwheels.

Descend to the A429, turn briefly right along this towards Cirencester, and then turn left to **Bourton-on-the-Water**.

On August Bank Holiday Bourton-on-the-Water becomes home to one of the rare surviving games of **Medieval football**. The River Windrush forms the pitch (the goals are in the shin-deep river), but unlike most other surviving versions, the teams here are remarkably small – just six aside. However, spectators should expect to get wet! The pretty bridges over the river have given rise to the description of Bourton-on-the-Water as the 'Venice of the Cotswolds'.

▸ Follow the High Street though the village centre and out to a T-junction by the post office. Turn right towards The Rissingtons, cross the River Dikler and turn right to **Great Rissington**. Continue on the major road past the Lamb Inn, bending left and uphill. After about

You should detour even if you don't wish to ride through the shallow ford, as it is very pretty!

It's well worth another quick detour along the riverside here.

Off-road riders may prefer to follow the start of Route 7 – via Wyck and Upper Rissington – here but in wet conditions, beware of deep rutted mud near Wyck Rissington.

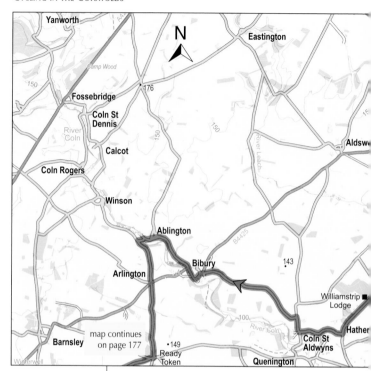

650m further, turn right at a T-junction, towards The Barringtons, and continue on this road for roughly 3.7km, descending past the deer park into **Great Barrington**.

Off-road route to Great Barrington

As you pass the Lamb Inn in Great Rissington, the off-road route turns right onto a minor road and heads downhill. Don't get too carried away with this downhill; part-way down, turn left onto a slightly hidden dead-end road by Holly Cottage, which rapidly becomes a track. Follow this straight ahead for about a kilometre until it bends abruptly right (SP 198 161).

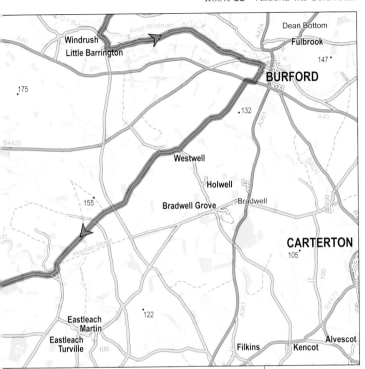

Continue straight ahead here along a grassy field edge to the left of a narrow strip of woodland, and go

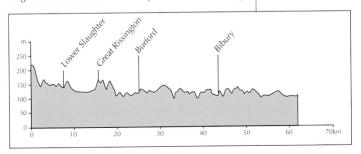

through a small wooden gate at the field's end. Now descend and go across a junction of tracks onto a more defined vehicle track. Follow this steeply down a dip and up the far side and continue to meet a road on a junction with a dead-end lane.

Turn right along the road and descend past the deer park into **Great Barrington**.

> The ruins of two former Roman villas nearby suggest **Great Barrington** has been an agricultural settlement since Roman times. It is one of several Cotswolds villages listed in the Domesday Book. The Barrington Estate (like many in the Cotswolds) was once part of a monastic estate – in this case Llanthony Priory. After dissolution it eventually passed into the Bray family, who are thought to have created the deer park in the 17th century.

Bend right by the war memorial, cross over both braids of the river and go past The Fox Inn, bending right and going uphill through **Little Barrington**. Partway up the hill turn left towards Burford. Overall descending,

Rolling countryside near Burford

this country lane undulates for roughly 4km to reach a T–junction just outside the village. Turn left and descend to the Lamb Inn. ▶

Take the road opposite the Lamb Inn (Tanners Lane), rising uphill to reach a busy main road (A40). This crossing is awkward: cycle along the main road for roughly 200m, heading right then left onto a quiet single-track lane towards Westwell. Turn right at a T-junction towards Aldsworth to enter the hamlet of **Westwell**, then stay on the major road for roughly 2.5km to reach a major crossroads. Cross over this and continue over two dips (the second, across the River Leach valley, is quite steep). Near the top of the re-ascent, turn right towards Hatherop then left at an oblique junction. Continue ahead for

It's worth a detour into the historic town of Burford before returning to this point.

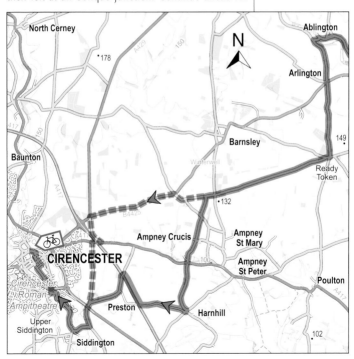

177

This is Akeman Street – a former Roman road linking Watling Street (near St Albans) with the Fosse Way (near Cirencester).

roughly 3.8km to **Hatherop**, bending left by Williamstrip Lodge. ◄ As you enter the village turn right to Coln St Aldwyns. Enjoy a descent and then rise gently into the centre of **Coln St Aldwyns**.

> The **school** on your left as you descend was once a medieval stately home and seat of the Hatherop Estate. Former owners include Maharajah Duleep Singh – the last King of the Sikh Empire – in the 19th century, and the state during WWII; one of its former owners established an early correspondence school, which was acquired by the forerunner of the current preparatory school.

Continue just past a conker tree in the centre of a junction and turn right then left to Bibury. Turn left at an oblique T-junction on the edge of **Bibury** and then descend on the major road to run next to the pretty river. Where the road bends sharp left across the river by the Swan Inn, turn right to Ablington. In **Ablington** turn left towards Winson, cross the River Coln, then turn left at a T-junction towards Barnsley. Continue for just over 1km

Bridge over the River Coln in Ablington

then cross over a five-way junction towards Poulton. A further 2km brings you to a crossroads at **Ready Token**.

Turn right (initially towards Barnsley) and then stay on the major road for roughly 3.5km. You are now on another long, straight stretch of Akeman Street. Pass a minor crossroads and take the next left (unsigned).

> **Road bikes** should continue to meet the B4425, head W along this and then S from a traffic light-controlled crossroads with the A429, taking a dog-leg right then left across the A417.

Dog-leg left then right across a major lane, continuing to reach a triangular green in the village of **Ampney Crucis**. Turn right and go past the Crown of Crucis Country Inn to reach a junction with the A417.

Cross this towards Driffield and then turn right at a T-junction towards Preston. Turn right again almost immediately onto a dead-end country lane, which ends where the ring road (also A417!) cuts it off. Turn right here onto a grassy bridleway, which narrows very quickly then joins a tarmac track after roughly 500m. This eventually bends left to join a country lane. Turn left and cross a bridge over the ring road.

Continue through **Preston**; as you exit the village turn left towards Cirencester. Cross over the main road (A419) almost immediately ahead. ▸ Shortly after a house called The Dairy Barn turn right to Siddington and go across the River Churn.

In **Siddington** turn right onto Ashton Road. Follow this into the outskirts of Cirencester; when through traffic is signposted left around a bend, go straight ahead onto the dead-end continuation of Siddington Road. Take the next left onto Kingsmead and use a narrow underpass to cross the dual carriageway. Rejoin the road opposite Kwik-Fit and turn right. Stay on the major road as it bends left, continuing past a couple of schools.

Roughly 150m after the second school (Paternoster), before some traffic lights, turn right onto The Avenue. Take the next left onto Tower Street and go over a major

This is more straightforward than it first appears.

The garden terrace at the Old Brewhouse B&B

crossroads onto South Way, now following brown signs towards Corinium Museum. This twists and turns; just beyond The Bear Inn turn left at a T-junction onto Dyer Street, heading back to Market Place. (For the Old Brewhouse B&B turn right and follow Dyer Street to a crossroads – the Old Brewhouse is just beyond.)

DAY 4
Cirencester to Stroud

Start	Traffic lights at the west end of Market Place, Cirencester (SP 023 020)
Finish	Stroud railway station (back entrance onto Cheapside, SO 849 051)
Distance	53km (33 miles)
Total ascent/descent	660m/725m
Grade	Moderate
Terrain	100% roads (optional off-road detour between Kingscote and Horsley)
Refreshments	On route: wide choice in Cirencester, Tetbury, Nailsworth and Stroud Short detour: The Bell PH (Sapperton)
Accommodation	The centre of Stroud has surprisingly little tourist accommodation, which almost certainly means you'll need to climb an extra hill if you want accommodation at the start or finish of the route! That said, it's worth the extra effort to get to Amberley Common (6km south of Stroud) for the views and for a friendly, reasonably-priced and comfortable 'pub with food and rooms' at the Amberley Inn. For campers the best options may be Seven Acres (CS, 7km northeast of Stroud) or the small but friendly Tobacconist Farm at Minchinhampton (7km southeast of Stroud).
Note	The optional off-road descent from Kingscote gets muddy more quickly than average in wet conditions. If it's been raining for a moderate period of time, and mud isn't your favourite surface, you may wish to take the road route regardless of the type of bike you're riding.

This may be the easiest day of the trip. It takes you on a slightly roundabout route via the historic wool town of Tetbury and brings you back to Stroud on straightforward sections of cycle path. The hills on this route are steep but short.

At the traffic lights turn right onto West Market Street. Pass a narrowing and continue as the road makes a sharp bend right and becomes Spitalgate Lane. At another traffic light-controlled crossroads continue straight ahead onto the 'White Way', following NCN48 for roughly 2.5km before bending right to cross a dual carriageway on a flyover. Take the next left towards **Perrots Brook**, descending to a junction with the A435.

Take a dog-leg left then right across this towards Daglingworth. Head steeply uphill on the major road

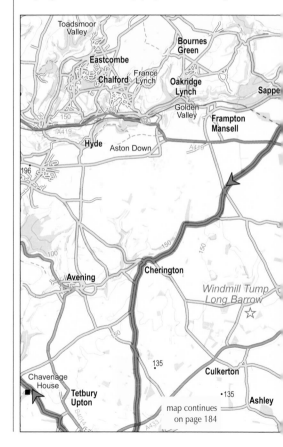

map continues
on page 184

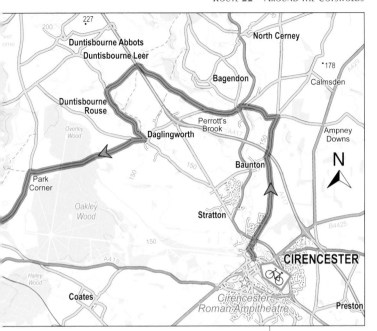

and at the top of the rise bear right (unsigned). This road eventually bends sharp left and goes under the A417 (roughly 2.3km from the A435 junction). Descend,

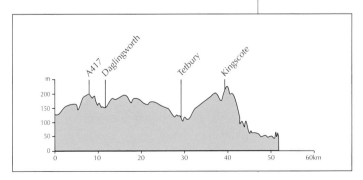

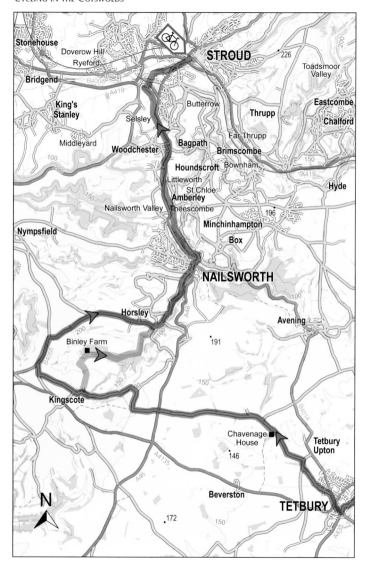

increasingly steeply, to cross a very quiet and rural valley with a ford in the bottom, then rise extremely steeply (but briefly) on the far side to a T-junction. Turn left and go along this quiet rural lane for nearly 2km to a T-junction in **Daglingworth**. Turn right and head gently uphill for nearly 3.5km to **Park Corner**.

> Park Corner would appear to be so-named as it's at the corner of **Cirencester Park**, part of the Earl of Bathurst's Estate. Sadly cycles appear to be excluded from this estate, so if you wish to detour en-route (open to walkers daily), you will need to do so on foot.

Turn left at the T-junction and continue for nearly 2km to pass close to **Sapperton**. Now follow signs for Cherington for roughly the next 6.5km. During this, go over a major crossroads leading to a pleasant dip and short re-ascent, then cross the A419 before contouring across a major road on a slightly oblique angle. At a T-junction on the edge of **Cherington** turn right towards Tetbury and bend left through the village. Continue on the major road for nearly 4.5km to the A433, crossing this with a slight dog-leg left then right onto Cirencester Road.

Continue all the way into **Tetbury** through a traffic-calmed area and up a hill into The Chipping. Continue along Chipping Street and turn right at the roundabout by The Snooty Fox PH onto Long Street. Where this bends sharp right on a junction take the second left towards Chavenage on the B4014. Continue past the entrance to the rugby ground and immediately after this fork left into Chavenage Lane (do not follow the brown signs to Chavenage House).

Ignore all side-turns before the entrance to Chavenage House (open Thursdays and Sundays 2.00pm–5.00pm, May to October). Continue past the house and through a tree-lined avenue in Chavenage Green, taking the left fork where the avenue splits and eventually reaching the **A46**.

Ripening crops surround the lane up to Hazlecote Farm

Cross this onto an access road to Hazlecote Farm, bending sharp right just in front of the farm. Turn left at the next junction (by a white trig point set in the wall) and descend past a few houses before climbing moderately steeply into **Kingscote**. Continue through the village, bending right past the church. Turn right towards 'The Windmill' as the road bends sharp left. Now turn right at two T-junctions to reach the B4058. Turn right along this and descend to Horsley.

Off-road alternative: Kingscote to Horsley
Turn right as you enter the village (towards Binley Farm), continuing ahead on a bridleway running over a private lane, then bend right then left on a deviation of the bridleway around the buildings of Hill Barn Farm. Descend to rejoin the farm track.

Near the bottom of the valley turn right by a wooden marker in front of the farm houses (but don't cross the stream) and follow a track into pasture. After roughly 350m bear left onto a faint but quite wide grassy track and descend through a small gate into woodland. A narrow track soon becomes a vehicle track, which is a bit rough and steep in a couple of places on the descent to a junction of tracks (roughly 1km after entering the

woodland). Continue straight ahead (don't cross the stream here), following bridleway markers. The track now undulates but overall descends gently to pass a few houses, then it bends right and rises again to a few more houses at the edge of Horsley. Turn left as another tarmac lane rises from the right, then turn right and immediately right again to emerge onto the B4058.

Descend, moderately steeply at first, and as you pass the Nailsworth village sign (near Pike Cottage) turn left and go briefly uphill along Horsley Road. This then descends quite steeply to a T-junction; turn right and descend to a further T-junction by The Britannia PH. Turn right and then bend left onto Old Market. At the end, turn right to reach a roundabout by a stone clock tower.

Turn left onto the A46 and use the filter lane to turn right by Egypt Mill. Follow this road as it bends left past the fire station and gently descend the valley to Stroud on a 'rail-trail' cycleway. The way is navigationally simple for the next 5km, but beware of occasional road/access track crossings.

Roughly 100m before a corrugated tin tunnel (SO 836 043), turn right to Stroud. Follow the cycle path through a residential area (bending right to cross a

The descent from Hill Barn Farm towards Binley Farm

There is no access from the next road back onto the track if you're tempted to detour left via the main road.

stream, then going straight ahead at road crossings) to a toucan crossing over a main road (A46). Use this, then haul the bike up a set of steps using a wheel-track on the right. ◄ Continue under a bridge. Roughly 120m after two bridges in quick succession, the tarmac does a sharp bend left and doubles back on itself to rise steeply up to a road (Rodborough Hill).

A cycle track continues on the pavement to the right (don't cross the road). Just before the road reaches a roundabout, bear right onto Wallbridge and go under a subway. Emerge onto a cut-off road near the Lockkeeper's Café. Turn right onto a dead-end lane at a roundabout (onto Cheapside) and head back to the station.

The lawnmower was invented in Stroud by **Edwin Beard Budding** in 1830 – as a by-product of the cutting machines in the woollen mills which trimmed the nap of the cloth. Lawns were now no longer the preserve of those with a flock of sheep to 'mow' them, or the super-rich who could afford full-time gardeners to scythe them.

APPENDIX A

Route summary table

No	Start	Distance	Grade	Ascent	% Road/Trail/Off-road	Page
1	Shipston-on-Stour	23km (14 miles)	Easy	260m	100/0/0	31
2	Shipston-on-Stour	24km (15 miles)	Easy	255m	81/0/19	35
3	Shipton-under-Wychwood	22km (14 miles)	Easy	270m	82/0/18	40
4	Bourton-on-the-Water	23km (14 miles)	Easy	300m	61/0/39	44
5	Alderton	35km (22 miles)	Moderate	215m	93/3/4	49
6	Bradford on Avon	34km (21 miles)	Variable	315m	13/87/0	54
7	Bourton-on-the-Water	26km (16 miles)	Moderate	415m	70/0/30	60
8	Kemble	32km (20 miles)	Moderate	120m	77/0/23	65
9	Kingham	28km (18 miles)	Moderate	255m	64/0/36	70
10	Batheaston	14km (9 miles)	Moderate	440m	100/0/0	76
11	Stratford-upon-Avon	42km (25 miles)	Moderate	320m	61/35/4	80
12	Cirencester	33km (21 miles)	Moderate	300m	94/0/6	85

No	Start	Distance	Grade	Ascent	% Road/Trail/Off-road	Page
13	Filkins	37km (23 miles)	Moderate	310m	67/0/33	90
14	Fairford	39km (24 miles)	Moderate	335m	69/0/31	96
15	Frampton Cotterell	44km (28 miles)	Moderate	455m	91/0/9	101
16	Stonehouse	43km (27 miles)	Moderate	450m	76/24/0	108
17	Stow-on-the-Wold	35km (22 miles)	Challenging	635m	63/0/37	115
18	Burford	43km (27 miles)	Challenging	470m	79/0/21	122
19	Stroud	66km (41 miles)	Challenging	1000m	100/0/0	129
20	Cheltenham	52km (33 miles)	Challenging	1010m	95.5/3/1.5	139
21	Malmesbury	48km (30 miles)	Challenging	430m	75/0/25	147
22	Stroud	209km (130 miles)	Moderate/Challenging	3100m	98/0/2	154
	Day 1: Stroud	47km (29 miles)	Challenging	1040m	100/0/0	156
	Day 2: Winchcombe	46km (29 miles)	Challenging	790m	98/0/2	163
	Day 3: Stow-on-the-Wold	63km (39 miles)	Moderate	610m	99/0/1	171
	Day 4: Cirencester	53km (33 miles)	Moderate	660m	100/0/0	181

APPENDIX B
Cycle hire and cycle shops

Notable closed times are mentioned where known, but this information was not available for all establishments and in any case is subject to change over time.

Mobile service (delivered to you)
Bourton-on-the-Water
Bourton Cycles: see main listing under hire centres below (covers Winchcombe/Chipping Campden/Bibury)

Chipping Norton
TY Cycles (covers most of Cotswolds)
Tel 07850 361146 or 01608 642765
enquiries@tycycles.co.uk
www.tycycles.co.uk

Stroud
The Bike Works: see main listing under Stroud (delivery charge per mile)

Somerford Keynes
Go by Cycle: see main listing under Cotswold Water Park (delivery charge per mile)

Hire centres
Bourton-on-the-Water
Bourton Cycles
2 Bourton Link
Bourton Industrial Park
GL54 2HQ
Tel 01451 822323 or 07917 634596
info@bourtoncycles.co.uk
www.bourtoncycles.co.uk (shop)

Hartwells Cotswold Cycle Hire
High Street
GL54 2AJ
Tel 01451 820405
hartwells@supanet.com
www.hartwells.supanet.com

Bath
Bath and Dundas Canal Co
Brassknocker Basin
Dundas Aqueduct
Monkton Combe
BA2 7JD
Tel 01225 722292
enquiries@bathcanal.com
www.bathcanal.com

Bradford on Avon
Towpath Trail Hire@TT Cycles
Frome Road
BA15 1LE
Tel 01225 867187
towpathtrail@ttcycles.co.uk
www.towpathtrail.co.uk (shop)

Bristol
Webbs of Warmley
14 High Street
Warmley
BS15 4ND
Tel 0117 9673676
info@webbsofwarmley.com
www.webbsofwarmley.co.uk (shop)

Bristol Cycle Shack
28 Midland Road
St Philips
BS2 0JY
Tel 0117 9299143 or 07816 934483
info@autp.co.uk
www.bristol-cycle-shack.co.uk (shop)

Jake's Bikes
6A Haymarket Walk
BS1 3LN
Tel 0117 3297363
www.jakesbikes.co.uk/hire (shop)

Blackboy Hill Cycles
180 Whiteladies Road
Clifton
BS8 2XU
Tel 0117 9731420
black_boy_cycles@hotmail.co.uk
www.blackboycycles.co.uk (shop)

Chippenham (Lacock)

History on your Handlebars
The Barn
Notton Park
Lacock
SN15 2NG
Tel 01249 730013 or 07855 810320
enquiries@historyonyour
hhandlebars.co.uk
www.historyonyourhandlebars.co.uk

Chipping Campden

Cycle Cotswolds
The Volunteer Inn
Lower High Street
GL55 6DY
Tel 01789 720193 or 07933 368074
info@cyclecotswolds.co.uk
www.cyclecotswolds.co.uk

Cheltenham

Compass Holidays
Cheltenham Spa Railway Station
Gloucester Road
GL51 8NP
Tel 01242 250642
info@compass-holidays.com
www.compass-holidays.com (they do
hire to the general public as well as to
those on their organised tours)

Cotswold Water Park (Somerford Keynes)

Go-By-Cycle
Tall Trees
Water Lane
Somerford Keynes
GL7 6DS
Tel 01285 862152 or 07970 419208
bev@go-by-cycle.co.uk
www.go-by-cycle.co.uk (shop; mobile
service also available)

Lechlade (Filkins)

Cotswold Woollen Weavers
Filkins
GL7 3JJ
Tel 01367 860660
info@naturalbest.co.uk
www.cotswoldwoollenweavers.co.uk
(select 'Visit' from the menu at the top
of the homepage)

Moreton-in-Marsh

The Toy Shop
High Street
GL56 0AD
Tel 01608 650756
www.thetoyshopmoreton.co.uk (closed
Tuesdays and Sundays; hybrid bikes
only)

Oxford

Bainton Bikes
78 Walton Street
OX2 6EA
Tel 01865 311610 or 07969 295502
info@baintonbikes.com
www.baintonbikes.com

Slimbridge

Slimbridge Boat Station
Shepherds Patch
GL2 7BP
Tel 01453 899190

Stonehouse
Mo's Bike Shed
Bonds Mill Estate
GL10 3RF
Tel 07738 055479
www.cyclehireingloucestershire.co.uk

Stroud
The Bike Works
Frogmarsh Mill
South Woodchester
GL5 5ET
Tel 01453 872824
info@thebikeworks.co.uk
www.thebikeworks.co.uk (closed
Sundays and Mondays; shop; mobile
service also available)

Stroud (Painswick)
Painswick Pedals
Painswick Rococo Garden
GL6 6TH
Tel 01452 813204
info@rococogarden.org.uk
www.painswickpedals.co.uk (electric
bikes only)

Stratford
Stratford Bike Hire
Railway Carriages
The Greenway
Seven Meadows Road
CV37 6GR
Tel 07711 776340
www.stratfordbikehire.com

Cycle shops/maintenance (only)
Beckford
Bredon Hill Bikes
Old Station Yard
GL20 7AN
Tel 07927 396575
www.bredonhillbikes.co.uk

Brimscombe
Noahs Ark Bikes
Bourne Mills
GL5 2TA
Tel 01453 884738
www.noahsark.co.uk

Cheltenham
Cheltenham Cycles
61 Winchcombe Street
GL52 2NE
Tel 01242 255414
info@cheltenhamcycles.co.uk
www.cheltenhamcycles.co.uk

Roylan Cycles
2 Suffolk Parade
GL50 2AB
Tel 01242 235948
www.roylancycles.co.uk

Chipping Sodbury
Blast Bikes
21 Horse Street
BS37 6DA
Tel 01454 319122
info@blastbikes.co.uk
www.blastbikes.co.uk

Cirencester
Independent Bikeworks
Unit 3
The Exchange
Brewery Court
GL7 1JL
Tel 01285 238184
info@independent-works.co.uk
www.independent-works.co.uk

Ride 24/76
The Wool Market
GL7 2PR
Tel 01285 642247
www.ride-247-cirencester.co.uk

Evesham
About Bikes
Orleans Close
Davies Road
WR11 2FP
Tel 01386 41444
info@about-bikes.com
www.about-bikes.com

Gloucester
Mitchells Cycles
260 Barton Street
GL1 4JJ
Tel 01452 411888
cyclesglos@btconnect.com
www.mitchellscycles.co.uk

Stratford-upon-Avon
The Cycle Studio
Guild Street
CV37 6QY
Tel 01789 205057
info@thecyclestudio.co.uk
www.thecyclestudio.co.uk

Stroud
Cytek
59 Westward Rd
GL5 4JA
Tel 01453 753330
www.cytekcycles.co.uk

Witney
Giles Cycles
1 Alvescot Road
Carterton
OX18 3JL
Tel 01993 842396
info@gilescycles.com
www.gilescycles.com

Yate
Terry's Cycles
44 Station Road
BS37 4PW
Tel 01454 318938
terryscycles@msn.com
www.bristolcycles.com

APPENDIX C
Cycles and trains

The routes in this guidebook have been designed with rail travel in mind. Many of the places provide a convenient starting point whether you arrive by vehicle or by train.

Those who have encountered efficient and user-friendly facilities for taking cycles on trains in other countries should beware of Britain's notoriously inconsistent – and often user-hostile – offering!

Typical cycle-transport issues

Different train operating companies often have different and conflicting policies regarding cycles.

- A single rail route may be used by two or more companies with different policies.
- Cycles are commonly limited to two per train.
- Tandems are very rarely carried at all.
- Cycles often need to be reserved in advance on specific trains.
- Internet and telephone services for general ticket sales are unable to perform cycle reservations; you may need to visit a station in person, with the ticket you bought online, to make a cycle reservation.
- Some services, by contrast, are non-reservable, the spaces being filled on a first-come, first-served basis.
- A non-reservable first stage of your journey may jeopardise later connections requiring a reservation.
- Oh, and don't even think about taking a bike onto a bus!

However, you will in practice find that long journeys can be completed successfully with a little patience, and that the strict company policies are in practice often implemented much more leniently by their staff on the ground.

National Rail provides a useful leaflet detailing options for carrying cycles on trains. Go to www.nationalrail.co.uk and look for the 'Cyclists' page, currently under 'Stations & on train'. You can download the leaflet from there.

The A to B website is also a useful source of current train operators' cycle policies, and it gives some hints on which are more cycle-friendly than others! Go to www.atob.org.uk and look for the 'UK Bike/Rail Restrictions' section, currently under 'Rail +'.

Train services to/from and within the Cotswolds (summer 2013)
From London
First Great Western trains run from London Paddington to Cheltenham Spa via Swindon, Stroud and Gloucester.

First Great Western trains run from London Paddington towards Hereford via Oxford, Charlbury, Kingham and Moreton-in-Marsh.

From Bristol
First Great Western trains run to Worcester via Yate, Cam and Dursley, Gloucester and Cheltenham.

Between Bristol and Birmingham
Cross Country operates a line via Cheltenham and Gloucester.

From Birmingham
London Midland runs a line to Stratford-upon-Avon.

Chiltern Railways operate a line from Warwick.

Train operating companies
First Great Western
www.firstgreatwestern.co.uk
Tel 08457 000125

Reservation strongly recommended at least 24hrs in advance on high-speed train services (limit of six bikes); on other services reservations are often not possible (limit of two bikes, first-come first-served).

Chiltern Railways
www.chilternrailways.co.uk
Tel 08456 005165

Reservation not possible in advance; space may be available for up to 10 bikes; first-come first-served.

London Midland
www.londonmidland.com
Tel 0844 8110133 (or 0121 6342040 from a mobile)
No reservation required.

Cross Country
www.crosscountrytrains.co.uk
Tel 0844 8110124

Reservation compulsory; two bikes only per train.

APPENDIX D

First aid for bike and rider

A crippling cycle breakdown can be very disheartening when its repair could be done simply with the correct tools, but there's always a balance to be struck against the weight of your toolkit. Punctures are by far the most likely cause of breakdown for a well maintained bike. The Cotswolds are quite a densely-populated area, as well as being popular with visitors, so you will rarely be far from some form of assistance in the event of an unrepairable breakdown.

The first few items below, marked with an asterisk, should be considered essential for all rides, whereas the later items may be more useful on longer (multi-day) or more challenging trips:

- *Set of three tyre levers
- *Spare inner tube – of the same size and valve type as your tyres.
- *Pump. Some pumps require a separate screw-on connector tube to connect to the valve on the tyre; there are two different types of connector for the two different valve types. Other pumps directly push onto the valve and need to be partly dismantled to change between the two different valve types. Either way, make sure you can use your pump to inflate your tyres.
- *Multi-adjustment spanner (particularly to enable non-quick-release wheels to be removed and to tighten luggage rack and mudguard nuts – these can work loose very quickly under touring conditions).
- Puncture repair kit (in case you get more than one puncture) containing sandpaper, vulcanising solution and patches.
- Set of allen keys (useful for securing the clamps at the ends of brake and gear cables (often 5mm), adjusting saddle height and angle/fore-aft position (often 6mm)).
- Screwdriver – useful for adjusting derailer gears and V-brakes (laterally).
- Tool to remove/replace/adjust brake pads (varies depending on brake type).

Various all-in-one tools combining a wide range of functions in a lightweight whole are now commonly available. If you're riding with others it can be tempting to save weight by sharing a toolkit, but remember that many of the items in the list may be specific to individual bikes.

Pre-ride checks for safety and enjoyment

You should perform the following basic tests before every ride:
- Tyres – check they are sufficiently inflated. There should be no or little depression when a tyre tread is pushed firmly with your thumb. There should be minimal visible 'bulge' on firm level ground when loaded with your weight.

- Brakes – check, when pushing by the handlebars, that each brake will easily apply to lock the wheel with plenty of remaining travel of the lever.
- Saddle – check that it is firmly attached and not able to move at all.
- Chain – check that this isn't rusty (orange or brown is a bad sign); oil or replace it if needed.
- Handlebars – with the front tyre gripped firmly between your knees, try to turn the handlebars. If they move, the headset needs tightening. This should only be attempted by the experienced.
- Wheels – check that quick-release levers are securely pushed home in the 'closed' position and the wheels do not wobble sideways when pushed.

How to change an inner tube

Although it is possible to repair a puncture on the route, it's much easier to exchange the punctured inner tube with a spare one and repair the puncture another time.

1   Look/listen for evidence of where the puncture is; remember its position relative to the valve.
2   Cycles with wide tyres and rim-operated brakes may need the brakes temporarily releasing, and so incorporate a mechanism to disengage the brake cable without tools.
3   Turn the bike upside-down and stand it on the saddle and handlebars, taking care not to damage any handlebar-mounted accessories.
4   Loosen the wheel by pulling the quick-release lever outwards through 180°, or by loosening the nuts on both sides if attached by nuts. With quick-release levers it may be necessary to loosen the thumb wheel on the other end of the axle to allow it to fully release from the frame.
5   Slide the wheel out of the frame and forks (wide tyres may need to be squeezed to pass between the brake pads).
6   Observe how the back wheel threads into the derailer and chain, and remember this for later.
7   Remove the valve cap and knurled nut (if any) from the valve stem. Release any remaining air pressure.
8   Starting away from the valve position and working towards the valve, use tyre levers to work one wall of the tyre out of the side of the wheel rim. Take care not to trap the tube as you do this. There is no need to fully remove the tyre from the wheel – just one sidewall.
9   Again starting away from the valve, pull the tube out from the tyre. Finishing at the valve, push the valve through the hole in the wheel rim and into the tyre so that it can be removed.

10   Locate the cause of the puncture by inspection or careful probing with the fingertips. Remove the cause (usually glass or a thorn) so you don't get a repeat puncture; the sharp end of a screwdriver or key can be useful to push it through the tread from the inside. Inexplicable punctures can be caused by hitting a sharp-edged stone (resulting in a 'snakebite' pair of punctures); valve failure; or by sharp edges in the wheel inadequately protected by the rim tape. Remember there may be multiple punctures.

(If don't have a spare tube you'll need to repair your punctured tube now.)

11   Slightly inflate the replacement tube so that it nearly holds its shape.
12   Reverse step 9 to put the tube back in the tyre and on the rim, starting with the valve.
13   Reverse step 8 to restore the tyre sidewall into the wheel rim, starting at the valve position. Take great care not to trap the tube between the wheel rim and tyre. Using tyre levers should not be necessary.
14   Re-fit knurled nut (if used) onto the stem of the valve; inflate the tyre until firm and replace the valve cap.
15   Return the wheel into the cycle frame. Front wheels are usually oriented with the quick-release lever on the left. Thread the back wheel back into the chain correctly. Take care not to dislodge brake pads, and that disc brakes locate correctly between the friction surfaces of the pads.
16   Secure the wheel. Quick-release mechanisms will need the thumb wheel tightening until the lever can be turned through 180°, offering increasingly firm resistance towards the end of its travel. The quick-release lever should end up firmly closed, parallel and close to the cycle frame but not touching it. Wheels with nuts should be tightened progressively on both sides.
17   Re-engage the brake cables if required.
18   Perform a full set of pre-ride checks (see above).

Basic first aid kit
This needs to be just large enough to treat the basics should one of the party come off the bike, without being overly heavy and cumbersome. Useful items include:
•   Disinfectant wipes
•   Plasters (various sizes)
•   Antiseptic cream
•   Wound pads/dressings (5cm+ sizes)
•   Wound closure strips
•   Small bandage
•   Small tweezers
•   Painkillers

Emergencies and first aid

In a life-threatening emergency:

- The first priority is to ensure that you and the casualty are not in further danger.
- Next, call for help (on 999 or 112).
- Then try and give whatever first aid is practical.

It is a life-threatening emergency if the casualty is not breathing or is unconscious/ unresponsive to their name.

The telephone number for the emergency services is 999. This will put you through to a combined control centre for ambulance, police and fire brigade services. 112, which is commonly used across Europe, will also get you through to the emergency services. The services will find it easier and quicker to get to the casualty if you can give them a good indication of where you are – a GPS location reading (in the OS map format, eg SP 123 456) can be very handy for this – and what the problem is (eg fallen off bike, hit head on kerb and is unconscious).

If you suspect the casualty has back or neck injuries **do not move them** unless their life is seriously threatened by remaining where they are; any movement may worsen the risk of paralysis. If you have no choice but to move them it is important to support their head (particularly) and back (also very important) fully while doing so – this may well require the help of more than one other person.

111 is the new number to call if the emergency is not life-threatening but still serious.

For minor injuries the first aid kit (you did bring it, didn't you?) will come in handy. If a cut that is bleeding significantly has gravel or any other object embedded in it, do not press on the foreign body directly but press at the sides of the wound to try and stem the bleeding. Then pile wound dressing on top of wound dressing with a bandage until blood flow from the wound becomes minimal, and seek help. For more minor cuts, bruises and gravel rash, plenty of antiseptic wipes, antiseptic cream, plasters and chocolate (for the casualty to eat!) should do the trick.

APPENDIX E
Other useful information

Tourist information centres
These are useful sources of information on accommodation and other activities/events taking place locally. They can be found across the region (Stratford-upon-Avon, Broadway, Moreton-in-Marsh, Winchcombe, Chipping Norton, Stow-on-the-Wold, Bourton-on-the-Water, Burford, Cheltenham, Stroud, Cirencester, Tetbury, Malmesbury, Yate, Chippenham and Bath).

Online information (general/events)
Cotswolds Tourism
www.cotswolds.com

Cotswold District Council
www.cotswold.gov.uk

The Cotswolds Stroud District
www.visitthecotswolds.org.uk

A Cotswolds Area of Outstanding Natural Beauty (AONB) sub-site
www.escapetothecotswolds.org.uk

Various independent sites such as
www.cotswolds.info
www.cotswoldevents.com
www.soglos.com and
www.cotswolds.org

Online information (accommodation)
General
Cyclists Welcome
www.cyclistswelcome.co.uk
Cyclists' Touring Club (CTC's) directory of cycle-friendly accommodation, cafés and bike shops

Beds for Cyclists
www.bedsforcyclists.co.uk
Independent accommodation information portalCotswolds B&Bs

www.cotswoldsbedbreakfasts.co.uk
Independent accommodation information portal

Camping
Camping and Caravanning Club
www.campingandcaravanningclub.co.uk

Includes approved campsite search tool

UK Campsite.co.uk
www.ukcampsite.co.uk
Directory of campsites and their facilities

Hostels
There are surprisingly few hostels in the region. Try:

YHA
www.yha.org.uk

Hostel Bookers
www.hostelbookers.com

DOWNLOAD THE ROUTES
IN GPX FORMAT

All the routes in this guide are available for download from:

www.cicerone.co.uk/CyclingCotswolds

as GPX files. You should be able to load them into most formats of mobile device, whether GPS or smartphone.

When you go to this link, you will be asked for your email address and where you purchased the guide, and have the option to subscribe to the Cicerone e-newsletter.

www.cicerone.co.uk

LISTING OF CICERONE GUIDES

BRITISH ISLES CHALLENGES, COLLECTIONS AND ACTIVITIES

The End to End Trail
The Mountains of England
 and Wales: 1&2
The National Trails
The Relative Hills of Britain
The Ridges of England, Wales
 and Ireland
The UK Trailwalker's Handbook
The UK's County Tops
Three Peaks, Ten Tors

UK CYCLING

Border Country Cycle Routes
Cycling in the Cotswolds
Cycling in the Hebrides
Cycling in the Peak District
Cycling in the Yorkshire Dales
Cycling the Pennine Bridleway
Mountain Biking in the
 Lake District
Mountain Biking in the Yorkshire
 Dales
Mountain Biking on the North
 Downs
Mountain Biking on the
 South Downs
The C2C Cycle Route
The End to End Cycle Route
The Lancashire Cycleway

SCOTLAND

Backpacker's Britain
 Central and Southern
 Scottish Highlands
 Northern Scotland
Ben Nevis and Glen Coe
Great Mountain Days
 in Scotland
Not the West Highland Way
Scotland's Best Small Mountains
Scotland's Far West
Scotland's Mountain Ridges
Scrambles in Lochaber
The Ayrshire and Arran
 Coastal Paths
The Border Country
The Cape Wrath Trail
The Great Glen Way
The Isle of Mull
The Isle of Skye
The Pentland Hills

The Scottish Glens 2 –
 The Atholl Glens
The Southern Upland Way
The Speyside Way
The West Highland Way
Walking Highland Perthshire
Walking in Scotland's Far North
Walking in the Angus Glens
Walking in the Cairngorms
Walking in the Ochils, Campsie
 Fells and Lomond Hills
Walking in Torridon
Walking Loch Lomond and
 the Trossachs
Walking on Harris and Lewis
Walking on Jura, Islay
 and Colonsay
Walking on Rum and the
 Small Isles
Walking on the Isle of Arran
Walking on the Orkney and
 Shetland Isles
Walking on Uist and Barra
Walking the Corbetts
 1 South of the Great Glen
 2 North of the Great Glen
Walking the Galloway Hills
Walking the Lowther Hills
Walking the Munros
 1 Southern, Central and
 Western Highlands
 2 Northern Highlands and
 the Cairngorms
Winter Climbs Ben Nevis and
 Glen Coe
Winter Climbs in the Cairngorms
World Mountain Ranges: Scotland

NORTHERN ENGLAND TRAILS

A Northern Coast to Coast Walk
Backpacker's Britain
 Northern England
Hadrian's Wall Path
The Dales Way
The Pennine Way

NORTH EAST ENGLAND, YORKSHIRE DALES AND PENNINES

Great Mountain Days in
 the Pennines
Historic Walks in
 North Yorkshire
South Pennine Walks
St Oswald's Way and

St Cuthbert's Way
The Cleveland Way and the
 Yorkshire Wolds Way
The North York Moors
The Reivers Way
The Teesdale Way
The Yorkshire Dales
 North and East
 South and West
Walking in County Durham
Walking in Northumberland
Walking in the North Pennines
Walks in Dales Country
Walks in the Yorkshire Dales
Walks on the North York Moors –
 Books 1 & 2

NORTH WEST ENGLAND AND THE ISLE OF MAN

Historic Walks in Cheshire
Isle of Man Coastal Path
The Isle of Man
The Lune Valley and Howgills
The Ribble Way
Walking in Cumbria's
 Eden Valley
Walking in Lancashire
Walking in the Forest of Bowland
 and Pendle
Walking on the West
 Pennine Moors
Walks in Lancashire
 Witch Country
Walks in Ribble Country
Walks in Silverdale and Arnside
Walks in the Forest of Bowland

LAKE DISTRICT

Coniston Copper Mines
Great Mountain Days in the Lake
 District
Lake District Winter Climbs
Lakeland Fellranger
 The Central Fells
 The Far-Eastern Fells
 The Mid-Western Fells
 The Near Eastern Fells
 The Northern Fells
 The North-Western Fells
 The Southern Fells
 The Western Fells
Roads and Tracks of the
 Lake District
Rocky Rambler's Wild Walks

Scrambles in the Lake District North & South
Short Walks in Lakeland
1 South Lakeland
2 North Lakeland
3 West Lakeland
The Cumbria Coastal Way
The Cumbria Way and the Allerdale Ramble
Tour of the Lake District

DERBYSHIRE, PEAK DISTRICT AND MIDLANDS
High Peak Walks
Scrambles in the Dark Peak
The Star Family Walks
Walking in Derbyshire
White Peak Walks
The Northern Dales
The Southern Dales

SOUTHERN ENGLAND
Suffolk Coast & Heaths Walks
The Cotswold Way
The North Downs Way
The Peddars Way and Norfolk Coast Path
The Ridgeway National Trail
The South Downs Way
The South West Coast Path
The Thames Path
Walking in Berkshire
Walking in Essex
Walking in Kent
Walking in Norfolk
Walking in Sussex
Walking in the Cotswolds
Walking in the Isles of Scilly
Walking in the New Forest
Walking in the Thames Valley
Walking on Dartmoor
Walking on Guernsey
Walking on Jersey
Walking on the Isle of Wight
Walks in the South Downs National Park

WALES AND WELSH BORDERS
Backpacker's Britain – Wales
Glyndwr's Way
Great Mountain Days in Snowdonia
Hillwalking in Snowdonia
Hillwalking in Wales: 1&2
Offa's Dyke Path

Ridges of Snowdonia
Scrambles in Snowdonia
The Ascent of Snowdon
The Ceredigion and Snowdonia Coast Paths
Lleyn Peninsula Coastal Path
Pembrokeshire Coastal Path
The Severn Way
The Shropshire Hills
The Wye Valley Walk
Walking in Pembrokeshire
Walking in the Forest of Dean
Walking in the South Wales Valleys
Walking on Gower
Walking on the Brecon Beacons
Welsh Winter Climbs

INTERNATIONAL CHALLENGES, COLLECTIONS AND ACTIVITIES
Canyoning
Europe's High Points
The Via Francigena (Canterbury to Rome): 1&2

EUROPEAN CYCLING
Cycle Touring in France
Cycle Touring in Ireland
Cycle Touring in Spain
Cycle Touring in Switzerland
Cycling in the French Alps
Cycling the Canal du Midi
Cycling the River Loire
The Danube Cycleway
The Grand Traverse of the Massif Central
The Rhine Cycle Route
The Way of St James

AFRICA
Climbing in the Moroccan Anti-Atlas
Kilimanjaro
Mountaineering in the Moroccan High Atlas
The High Atlas
Trekking in the Atlas Mountains
Walking in the Drakensberg

ALPS – CROSS-BORDER ROUTES
100 Hut Walks in the Alps
Across the Eastern Alps: E5
Alpine Points of View
Alpine Ski Mountaineering

1 Western Alps
2 Central and Eastern Alps
Chamonix to Zermatt
Snowshoeing
Tour of Mont Blanc
Tour of Monte Rosa
Tour of the Matterhorn
Trekking in the Alps
Trekking in the Silvretta and Rätikon Alps
Walking in the Alps
Walks and Treks in the Maritime Alps

PYRENEES AND FRANCE/SPAIN CROSS-BORDER ROUTES
Rock Climbs in the Pyrenees
The GR10 Trail
The Mountains of Andorra
The Pyrenean Haute Route
The Pyrenees
The Way of St James
Through the Spanish Pyrenees: GR11
Walks and Climbs in the Pyrenees

AUSTRIA
The Adlerweg
Trekking in Austria's Hohe Tauern
Trekking in the Stubai Alps
Trekking in the Zillertal Alps
Walking in Austria

EASTERN EUROPE
The High Tatras
The Mountains of Romania
Walking in Bulgaria's National Parks
Walking in Hungary

FRANCE
Chamonix Mountain Adventures
Ecrins National Park
GR20: Corsica
Mont Blanc Walks
Mountain Adventures in the Maurienne
The Cathar Way
The GR5 Trail
The Robert Louis Stevenson Trail
Tour of the Oisans: The GR54
Tour of the Queyras
Tour of the Vanoise
Trekking in the Vosges and Jura

Vanoise Ski Touring
Via Ferratas of the French Alps
Walking in the Auvergne
Walking in the Cathar Region
Walking in the Cevennes
Walking in the Dordogne
Walking in the Haute Savoie
North & South
Walking in the Languedoc
Walking in the Tarentaise and
Beaufortain Alps
Walking on Corsica

GERMANY

Germany's Romantic Road
Hiking and Biking in the Black
Forest
Walking in the Bavarian Alps
Walking the River Rhine Trail

HIMALAYA

Annapurna
Bhutan
Everest
Garhwal and Kumaon
Kangchenjunga
Langtang with Gosainkund
and Helambu
Manaslu
The Mount Kailash Trek
Trekking in Ladakh
Trekking in the Himalaya

ICELAND & GREENLAND

Trekking in Greenland
Walking and Trekking in Iceland

IRELAND

Irish Coastal Walks
The Irish Coast to Coast Walk
The Mountains of Ireland

ITALY

Gran Paradiso
Sibillini National Park
Stelvio National Park
Shorter Walks in the Dolomites
Through the Italian Alps
Trekking in the Apennines
Trekking in the Dolomites
Via Ferratas of the Italian
Dolomites: Vols 1 & 2
Walking in Abruzzo
Walking in Sardinia
Walking in Sicily
Walking in the Central

Italian Alps
Walking in the Dolomites
Walking in Tuscany
Walking on the Amalfi Coast
Walking the Italian Lakes

MEDITERRANEAN

Jordan – Walks, Treks, Caves,
Climbs and Canyons
The Ala Dag
The High Mountains of Crete
The Mountains of Greece
Treks and Climbs in Wadi Rum
Walking in Malta
Western Crete

NORTH AMERICA

British Columbia
The Grand Canyon
The John Muir Trail
The Pacific Crest Trail

SOUTH AMERICA

Aconcagua and the
Southern Andes
Hiking and Biking Peru's
Inca Trails
Torres del Paine

SCANDINAVIA

Walking in Norway

SLOVENIA, CROATIA AND MONTENEGRO

The Julian Alps of Slovenia
The Mountains of Montenegro
Trekking in Slovenia
Walking in Croatia
Walking in Slovenia:
The Karavanke

SPAIN AND PORTUGAL

Costa Blanca: West
Mountain Walking in
Southern Catalunya
The Mountains of Central Spain
The Northern Caminos
Trekking through Mallorca
Walking in Madeira
Walking in Mallorca
Walking in Menorca
Walking in the Algarve
Walking in the Cordillera
Cantabrica
Walking in the Sierra Nevada
Walking on Gran Canaria
Walking on La Gomera and El

Hierro
Walking on La Palma
Walking on Tenerife
Walking the GR7 in Andalucia
Walks and Climbs in the
Picos de Europa

SWITZERLAND

Alpine Pass Route
Canyoning in the Alps
Central Switzerland
The Bernese Alps
The Swiss Alps
Tour of the Jungfrau Region
Walking in the Valais
Walking in Ticino
Walks in the Engadine

TECHNIQUES

Geocaching in the UK
Indoor Climbing
Lightweight Camping
Map and Compass
Mountain Weather
Moveable Feasts
Outdoor Photography
Polar Exploration
Rock Climbing
Sport Climbing
The Book of the Bivvy
The Hillwalker's Guide to
Mountaineering
The Hillwalker's Manual

MINI GUIDES

Alpine Flowers
Avalanche!
Navigating with a GPS
Navigation
Pocket First Aid and
Wilderness Medicine
Snow

MOUNTAIN LITERATURE

8000m
A Walk in the Clouds
Unjustifiable Risk?

For full information on all
our guides, and to order
books and eBooks, visit our
website:
www.cicerone.co.uk.

Walking – Trekking – Mountaineering – Climbing – Cycling

Over 40 years, Cicerone have built up an outstanding collection of 300 guides, inspiring all sorts of amazing adventures.

 Every guide comes from extensive exploration and research by our expert authors, all with a passion for their subjects. They are frequently praised, endorsed and used by clubs, instructors and outdoor organisations.

All our titles can now be bought as **e-books** and many as iPad and Kindle files and we will continue to make all our guides available for these and many other devices.

Our website shows any **new information** we've received since a book was published. Please do let us know if you find anything has changed, so that we can pass on the latest details. On our **website** you'll also find some great ideas and lots of information, including sample chapters, contents lists, reviews, articles and a photo gallery.

It's easy to keep in touch with what's going on at Cicerone, by getting our monthly **free e-newsletter**, which is full of offers, competitions, up-to-date information and topical articles. You can subscribe on our home page and also follow us on **Facebook** and **Twitter**, as well as our **blog**.

Cicerone – the very best guides for exploring the world.

CICERONE

2 Police Square Milnthorpe Cumbria LA7 7PY
Tel: 015395 62069 info@cicerone.co.uk
www.cicerone.co.uk